# READING AND WRITING Sourcebook

**Authors**

Robert Pavlik

Richard G. Ramsey

Great Source Education Group

a Houghton Mifflin Company

## Authors

**Richard G. Ramsey** is currently a national educational consultant for many schools throughout the country and serves as President of Ramsey's Communications. For more than twenty-three years he has served as a teacher and a principal for grades 1–12. Dr. Ramsey has also served on the Curriculum Frameworks Committee for the State of Florida. A lifelong teacher and educator and former principal, he is now a nationally known speaker on improving student achievement and motivating students.

**Robert Pavlik** taught high school English and reading for seven years. His university assignments in Colorado and Wisconsin have included teaching secondary/content area reading, chairing a Reading/Language Arts Department, and directing a Reading/Learning Center. He is an author of several books and articles and serves as the Director of the School Design and Development Center at Marquette University.

Printed in the United States of America.

International Standard Book Number: 0-669-47630-7

2 3 4 5 6 7 8 9 10 — BA — 06 05 04 03 02 01

# Table of Contents

## Table of Contents

# READING AND WRITING Sourcebook

# Responding to Literature

When you read, do you mark up the text? Do you circle unusual words or highlight important ideas? Active readers know how to respond to literature. They read with a pen in hand and use the margins to write notes and ask questions.

Becoming an active reader is easy. Read this poem. Then look at the way one reader has marked it up.

---

**RESPONSE NOTES**

**1. MARK**

**2. QUESTION**
How old is the speaker?

**3. CLARIFY**
Life = Big phase

**4. VISUALIZE**
Life ⟶ Death

**5. PREDICT**
Speaker will grow up even more.

**6. REACT AND CONNECT**
Sometimes I feel like this.

### "Thinking" by Lorna Dee Cervantes

I think I grew up last year.
Or maybe today
is just a <u>phase</u>,
 like Autumn's bright red <u>foliage</u>
 just before Winter's death.
Sometimes I think that maybe
life
is nothing but
one big phase
waiting for the next,
and death
is what you have
when you run out of phases.
I think that maybe
I did grow up . . .
some.

**VOCABULARY**
**phase**—stage; part of a process.
**foliage**—leaves.

---

# Response Strategies

There is not just one right way to respond to a text. Different readers will notice different words, question different ideas, or react to different scenes. Below are 6 general ways readers respond to literature.

## 1. Mark or highlight
Use a pen or highlighter to underline or circle words that are important or unusual. Marking part of a text makes it easier to find important passages when you reread or review.

## 2. Question
Ask questions as you read: "Do I agree with this?" or "Why did the character do that?" Questions trigger thoughts in your mind and keep you interested as a reader.

## 3. Clarify
Ask yourself what an author is trying to say. Put ideas in your own words or number parts of a plot or an argument. Active readers are always trying to make clear what they have read.

## 4. Visualize
When you read, you see in your mind pictures of what the writer is describing. Make sketches to help you visualize those mental images or use a chart or organizer to remember key ideas.

## 5. Predict
Guessing what will come next helps you follow a story or article more closely. Think about how a story will end or what an author's final point will be. Making predictions keeps active readers interested in what they're reading.

## 6. React and Connect
Active readers try to relate to what they're reading. Jot down your opinions and reactions in the margins of books. When you connect to the people and events you're reading about, you will get more from your reading.

As you read the selections in this *Sourcebook*, keep a pen or pencil handy. Use these strategies in the Response Notes space beside each selection.

Practice using some of the strategies with the poem fragment below. Read it 2 or 3 times. Use a different response strategy each time you reread.

## "I Belong" by A. Whiterock

All that I see around me
   I am a part of.

I am the mountain, to stand
   with pride, strength, and faith.
I am the tree, to stand tall and straight,
   above all to be honest with myself,
   and to my brothers and my sisters.

I am the grass, to show kindness and love
   to all who surround me and
   above all to love myself as well as others,
   to be more <u>considerate</u> of my
   brothers and my sisters.
To understand more clearly.

**VOCABULARY**
**considerate**—respectful; thoughtful.

# Family Matters

**F**amilies deal with all sorts of matters. They celebrate the births of children and mourn the deaths of relatives. When tragedy strikes or when good fortune shines down, it's comforting to have your family by your side.

What do you think of when you hear the word *father*? Sometimes our first thoughts are our finest ones. That's why it's important to get those thoughts down on paper before you forget them.

**BEFORE YOU READ**

Think for a moment about the word *father*. Then do a 1-minute quickwrite.

1. Write everything that comes to mind when you hear the word *father*.
2. Just keep writing. Don't stop to check spelling, grammar, or punctuation.

**1-MINUTE QUICKWRITE**

## II. READ

Now read "Father." Read with a pencil and marker in hand.

**1.** As you read, try to **visualize** the scenes and people the author describes.

**2.** In the Response Notes, make sketches of what you "see."

---

### "Father" from *Living up the Street*
by Gary Soto

My father was showing me how to water. Earlier in the day he and a friend had <u>leveled</u> the backyard with a <u>roller</u>, then with a <u>two-by-four</u> they dragged on a rope to fill in the depressed areas, after which they watered the ground and <u>combed</u> it slowly with a steel rake. They were preparing the ground for a new lawn. They worked shirtless in the late summer heat, and talked only so often, stopping now and then to point and say things I did not understand—how fruit trees would do better near the alley and how the vegetable garden would do well on the east side of the house.

"Put your thumb like this," he said. Standing over me, he took the hose and placed his thumb over the opening so that the water streamed out hissing and showed silver in

EXAMPLE:

**VOCABULARY**

**leveled**—flattened; evened out.
**roller**—heavy metal lawn tool that is pushed or pulled to smooth the ground.
**two-by-four**—piece of wood that is 2 inches thick and 4 inches wide.
**combed**—went over.

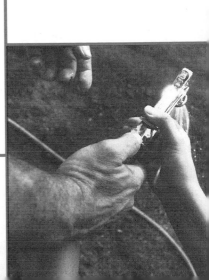

RESPONSE NOTES

that dusk. I tried it and the water hissed and went silver as I pointed the hose to a square patch of dirt that I soaked but was careful not to <u>puddle</u>.

**STOP AND RETELL**

What are they doing?

..............................................................................

..............................................................................

..............................................................................

Father returned to sit down with an iced tea. His knees were water-stained and his chest was <u>flecked</u> with mud. Mom sat next to him, garden gloves resting on her lap. She was wearing checkered shorts and her hair was tied up in a <u>bandanna</u>. He patted his lap, and she jumped into it girlishly, arms around his neck. They raised their heads to watch me—or look through me, as if something were on the other side of me—and talked about our new house, the neighbors, trees they would plant, the playground down the block. They were tired from the day's work but were happy. When Father pinched her legs, as if to <u>imply</u> they were fat, she punched him gently and played with his hair.

The water streamed, nickel-colored, as I slowly worked from one end to the next. When I raised my face to Father's to ask if I could stop, he pointed to an area that I had missed.

**VOCABULARY**
**puddle**—make a pool of water.
**flecked**—spotted.
**bandanna**—cloth or handkerchief worn on the head.
**imply**—say; suggest.

Although it was summer I was cold from the water and my thumb hurt from pressing the hose, <u>triggerlike</u>, to reach the far places. But I wanted to please him, to work hard as he had, so I watered the patch until he told me to stop. I turned off the water, <u>coiled</u> the hose as best I could, and sat with them as they talked about the house and stared at where I had been standing.

The next day Father was hurt at work. A neck injury. Two days later he was dead. I remember the hour—two in the afternoon. An uncle slammed open the back door at Grandma's and the three of us—cousin Isaac, Debbie, and I who were playing in the yard—grew stiff because we thought we were in trouble for doing something wrong. He looked at us, face <u>lined</u> with worry and shouting to hurry to the car. At the hospital I <u>recall</u> Mother holding her hand over her eyes as if she was looking into a light. She was leaning into someone's shoulder and was being led away from the room in which Father lay.

STOP AND RETELL

What big change suddenly occurred?

........................................................................

........................................................................

........................................................................

STOP AND RETELL

**VOCABULARY**
**triggerlike**—like pressing the trigger of a gun.
**coiled**—wound in a spiral.
**lined**—marked.
**recall**—remember.

I remember looking up but saying nothing, though I sensed what had happened—that Father was dead. I did not feel <u>sorrow</u> nor did I cry, but I felt <u>conspicuous</u> because relatives were pressing me against their legs or holding my hand or touching my head, tenderly. I stood among them, some of whom were crying while others had their heads bowed and mouths moving. The three of us were led away down the hall to a cafeteria where an uncle bought us candies that we ate standing up and looking around, after which we left the hospital and walked into a harsh afternoon light. We got into a blue car I had never seen before.

At the funeral there was crying. I knelt with my brother and sister, hands folded and trying to be patient, though I was itchy from the tiny coat whose shoulders worked into my armpits and from the heat of a stuffy car on our long and slow drive from the church in town. Prayers were said and a <u>eulogy</u> was given by a man we did not know. We were asked to view the <u>casket</u>, with our mother and the three of us to lead the <u>procession</u>. An uncle helped my mother while we walked shyly to view our father for the last time. When I stood at the casket, I was surprised to see him, eyes closed

**VOCABULARY**
**sorrow**—sadness.
**conspicuous**—obvious; easily noticed.
**eulogy**—speech praising the person who died.
**casket**—coffin.
**procession**—movement of people in an orderly way.

**"Father"** continued

and <u>moist</u>-looking and wearing a cap the color of skin. (Years later I would realize that it hid the wound from which he had died.) I looked quickly and returned to my seat, head bowed because my relatives were watching me and I felt scared.

We buried our father. Later that day at the house, Grandma could not stop shaking from her nerves, so a doctor was called. I was in the room when he opened his bag and shiny things <u>gleamed</u> from inside it. Scared, I left the room and sat in the living room with my sister, who had a doughnut in her hand, with one bite gone. An aunt whose face was twisted from crying looked at me and, feeling embarrassed, I lowered my head to play with my fingers.

**STOP AND THINK**

How does the narrator feel about the death of his father?

........................................................................................

........................................................................................

........................................................................................

A week later relatives came to help build the fence Father had planned for the new house. A week after that Rick, Debra, and I were playing in an <u>unfurnished</u>

**VOCABULARY**
**moist**—damp.
**gleamed**—shined; glistened.
**unfurnished**—empty; without furniture.

## RESPONSE NOTES

bedroom with a can of marbles Mother had given us. Behind the closed door we rolled the marbles so that they banged against the baseboard and jumped into the air. We separated, each to a corner, where we swept them <u>viciously</u> with our arms—the clatter of the marbles hitting the walls so loud I could not hear the things in my heart.

**VOCABULARY**
**viciously**—harshly.

## STOP AND RETELL STOP AND RETELL STOP AND RETELL

What happens in "Father"? Retell the story in the boxes below.

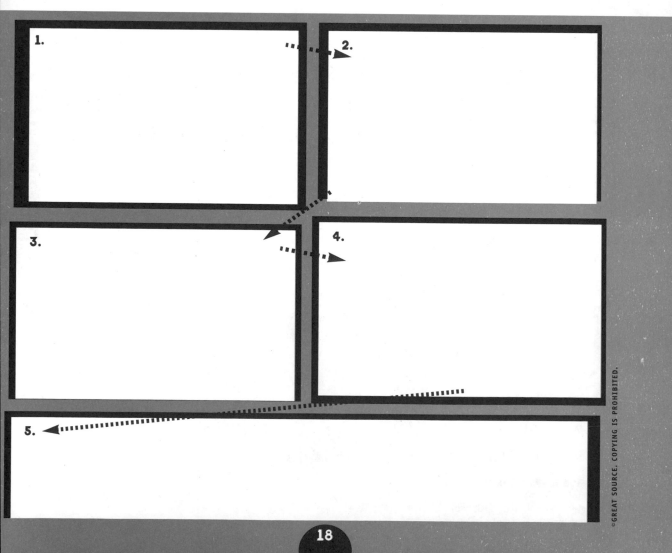

1.

2.

3.

4.

5.

## III. GATHER YOUR THOUGHTS

**A. CHOOSE A TOPIC** When you retell an event, you don't tell *everything*. You zoom in on the most important parts of the event.

**1.** In the circles, list 3 important events that have happened to your family.

**2.** Then describe each event underneath.

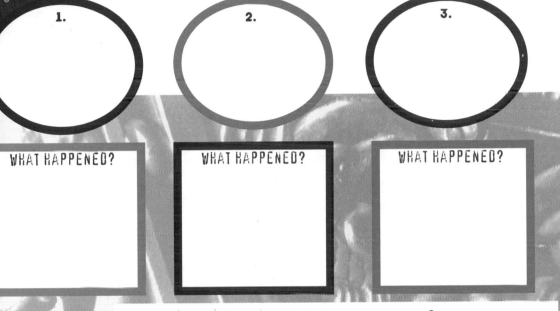

| 1. | 2. | 3. |

**WHAT HAPPENED?**      **WHAT HAPPENED?**      **WHAT HAPPENED?**

**B. NARROW YOUR FOCUS** Now narrow your focus.

**1.** Choose part of one of the events to write a paragraph about.

**2.** Then answer the questions.

My focus:

Who was there?

What happened?

Where and when did it occur?

How did I feel about it?

# IV. WRITE

Write a **paragraph** describing the event that happened to your family.

**1.** Include details from the previous page that tell what happened, when, where, and how you felt about it.

**2.** Use the Writers' Checklist to help you revise.

# V. WRAP-UP

What is the point, or main idea, of "Father"?

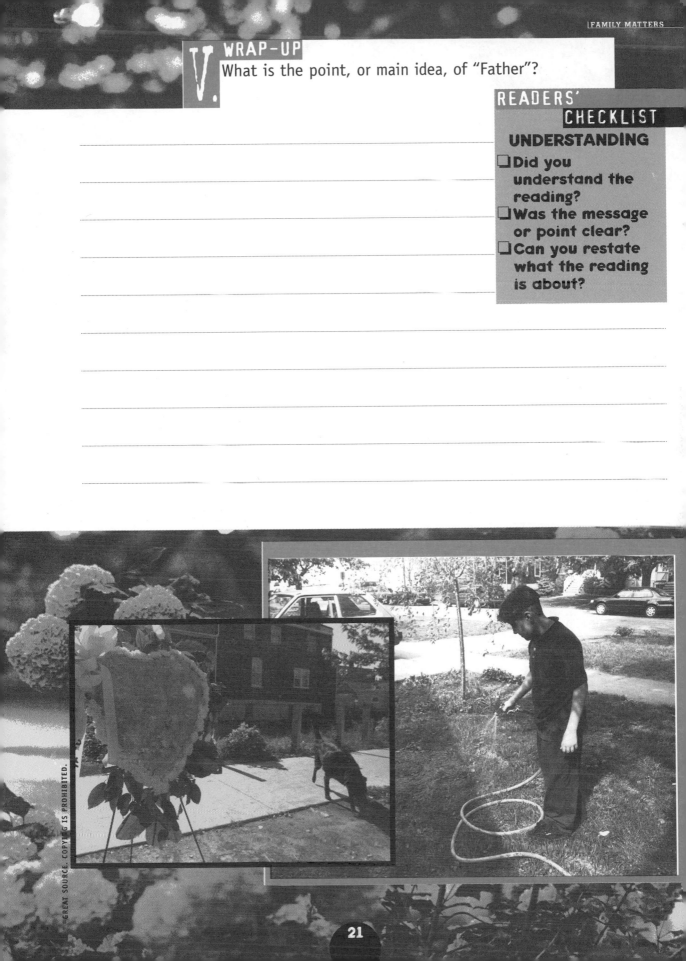

# 2: Mother

Have you ever felt an author wrote a story just for you? If so, it means you've made a connection to the writing. Your connections can help you better understand what you read.

## BEFORE YOU READ

Previewing what you read can help you connect to it. Read the title and look quickly through "Mother."
1. Underline 4–5 key words or phrases in both the first and the last paragraphs.
2. Then answer the questions below.

What do you think "Mother" is about?

How does the author feel about her mother?

When and where is this story set?

What kind of connections can you make to the story?

# II. READ

With a reading partner, take turns reading Baxter's memoir aloud.

1. **Connect** what's being described to your own feelings and experiences.
2. Jot down your **reactions** and thoughts in the Response Notes.

## "Mother" from *The Seventh Child*
## by Freddie Mae Baxter

When my mother had her children, she wanted all of them to be children, not boys and girls. Everybody could do the same thing. There wasn't no such thing as a boy job or a girl job. The boys had to do just what the girls did. And I liked her for that. She didn't say, "All right now, you boys cut the wood and you girls go and make up the beds." It didn't matter if it was a girl that cut the wood or a boy that cut the wood. Or the boy that made the bed or the girl that made the bed. Every one of my brothers could cook a meal, take care of their wife and their children, just like any woman; like they could put on diapers, comb the baby's hair. They could wash, iron, sew, cook. They could do everything for themselves. Every last one of Momma's children could do that. If they didn't want to get married, they didn't have to get married, because they could do everything for themselves.

EXAMPLE:
I wonder if the boys liked learning to do all this!

My mother told us this: Whatever you have, you make sure it's clean. My mother said some kids have three or four dresses but if you have just one dress, and if your one is standing out nice and clean and your skin is clean, you can beat out the others with three or four dresses because they are no cleaner than you are with one. That's why when I see a dirty person, I get angry.

STOP AND THINK

**What does Freddie's mother say about keeping clean?**

Saturday nights was our best time. I used to call Saturday and Sunday "colored people's days." You wasn't working then and you could get yourself together. Them boys would get their shirts clean: They would wash and <u>starch</u> and iron those shirts and go to see the little girls. Now I always say: Whatever you got, if you keep it clean, nobody don't know if you bought it yesterday, twenty years ago, or thirty years ago.

**VOCABULARY**
**starch**—stiffen with a powdery substance.

"Mother" continued

Whatever we had in our house, we would cook it and everybody would sit down together at the table. You put food on the table and you had to say grace before you ate it. And sometimes my mother would come with some more food. She would be working for the families and they have food left over. Sometimes she would come in with half of this and half of that that they didn't eat, because they didn't want no leftovers. Whatever they had that day, they didn't want for tomorrow. So my mother would bring it home and we would serve that too. What little food we had—it wasn't much, but we had enough.

**STOP AND THINK**

How does Freddie feel about her mother?

_____

_____

_____

Whatever we had we shared. It was eight of us so if there was food, everybody got a certain amount. It wasn't like you could go back and say, "I want some more." So you shared it. We didn't have anything to fight about because we didn't have anything. We were poor but we didn't have a bad life. You know you can have and not be happy and you cannot have and be happy. We just didn't have

**VOCABULARY**
grace—a prayer.

anything but we were happy. What we had, we ate and that was it.

If there was a piece of bread, we all shared that piece of bread together. Because nobody is gonna eat it all by themselves, they gonna fix it so somebody else gets some. If you didn't share, my mother would say something like, "You know you got enough there. You give her some." It's almost like a tree. You have a little tree and you bend it when it's small but you can't bend it after it grows up. Even if you ain't got nothing, if you got love you can almost produce something. But when you don't love, you can't share. In my family, we were taught to love. We were taught to take care of each other and love each other. We didn't have anything but we had lots of love.

STOP AND THINK STOP AND THINK STOP AND THINK

What is the author trying to express to readers?

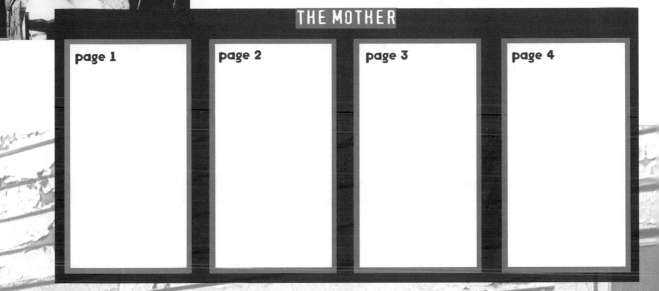

# III. GATHER YOUR THOUGHTS

**A. REFLECT** Reflect on how Baxter describes her mother.

**1.** Think of 1 idea you got about the mother from each page of the selection.

**2.** Write the word or phrase describing her in each box.

## THE MOTHER

| page 1 | page 2 | page 3 | page 4 |
| --- | --- | --- | --- |
| | | | |

**B. CHOOSE A TOPIC** Get ready to write a descriptive paragraph about a person who is important to you.

**1.** First choose the person you want to describe.

**2.** Then brainstorm 3–4 things that make this person special to you.

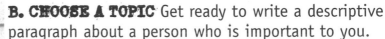

I want to describe

What makes this person special?

1.

2.

3.

4.

**C. PLAN YOUR PARAGRAPH** You'll need to plan the main idea and details for your paragraph.

**1.** Complete the topic sentence.

**2.** Then think of and write 3 details that explain the person's importance to you.

**3.** In the last box, tell how you feel about the person.

**TOPIC SENTENCE**

is special to me because

**DETAIL 1**

**DETAIL 2**

**DETAIL 3**

About this person, I feel . . .

# IV. WRITE

Now write a **descriptive paragraph** about a person who is special to you.

1. Begin with your topic sentence.
2. Then give details that support it. Start a new sentence for each detail.
3. Use the Writers' Checklist to help you revise.

## WRITERS' CHECKLIST

### SENTENCE FRAGMENTS

☐ Did you avoid writing sentence fragments? Fragments may begin with a capital letter and end with a period, but they are incomplete. You can fix fragments by adding a subject or a verb or by completing the thought. EXAMPLES: *Told us to do the wash.* (fragment) *My mother told us to do the wash.* (complete) *My sister and I laughing.* (fragment) *My sister and I laughed.* (complete)

## What did "Mother" mean to you?

_____

_____

_____

_____

_____

_____

_____

_____

_____

## READERS' CHECKLIST

**MEANING**

☐ Did you learn something from the reading?

☐ Did it affect you or make an impression?

# Whales

Whales are among the largest, most intelligent, and most mysterious creatures ever to have lived. Found in all the oceans of the world, whales spend their entire lives in water. While their grace, power, and beauty have captured our imaginations, scientists have much to learn about whales and their world.

# 3: The Great Whales

Whales are amazing! What do you know about them? You might be surprised by how much you know. Using a K-W-L chart will help you keep track of what you know and what you need to learn.

## BEFORE YOU READ

Fill in this K-W-L Chart.

1. Write what you know about whales in the **K** column.
2. Write what you want to find out in the **W** column. Save the **L** column for later.
3. Share what you know and your questions with your reading partner.

## K-W-L Chart

| WHAT I **K**NOW | WHAT I **W**ANT TO KNOW | WHAT I HAVE **L**EARNED |
|---|---|---|
| | | |

## READ

Now read this selection about whales.

**1.** As you're reading, think of questions you wrote in your K-W-L Chart. **Mark** or **highlight** information that helps answer them.

**2.** Write important or interesting details in the Response Notes.

**Response Notes**

### "The Great Whales" by Seymour Simon

The great whales are the world's giant animals. This humpback whale is breaching—jumping almost clear out of the water and then crashing down in a huge spray of foam. The humpback whale is longer than a big bus and heavier than a trailer truck. Some great whales are even larger. Just the tongue of a blue whale weighs as much as an elephant.

Whales are not fish, as some people mistakenly think. Fish are cold-blooded animals. This means their body temperature changes with their surroundings. Whales are mammals that live in the sea. Like cats, dogs, monkeys, and people, whales are warm-blooded. Their body temperature remains much the same—whether they swim in the icy waters of the Arctic or in warm tropical seas.

EXAMPLE:
whales =
warm-blooded
mammals

## stop+clarify

Is a whale a fish or a mammal? Explain how you know.

......................................

......................................

stop+clarify

**VOCABULARY**
breaching—leaping.
Arctic—one of the coldest regions in the world, located near the North Pole.

A fish breathes by taking in water and passing it through <u>gills</u> to <u>extract</u> oxygen, but a whale must <u>surface</u> to <u>inhale</u> air into its lungs. A whale's nostril, called a blowhole, is at the top of its head. A whale breathes through its blowhole. Some whales, such as the humpback, have two blowholes. Here they are open, as the humpback whale exhales old air and inhales fresh oxygen-rich air.

# stop+question

How does the humpback whale breathe?

........................................................................................

........................................................................................

# stop+question

The air that whistles in and out of a whale's blowhole moves at speeds of two or three hundred miles an hour. It enters and leaves the lungs, within the whale's chest. With each breath, a whale inhales thousands of times more air than you do. The whale closes its blowhole and holds its breath when it dives. Some kinds of whales can dive to depths as great as a mile and hold their breath for more than an hour during a deep dive. When they surface, they blow out a huge breath and then

**VOCABULARY**
**gills**—organs for breathing of most animals that live in water.
**extract**—get.
**surface**—rise to the top of the water.
**inhale**—breathe in.

take several smaller breaths before diving again.

A whale has a tail with <u>horizontal flukes</u>, which are different from the <u>vertical</u> tail fins of a fish. The fins of a fish have bones and move from side to side. Flukes have no bones and are moved up and down by powerful muscles connected to the whale's <u>spine</u>. The upward stroke of the tail pushes the whale through the water, sometimes at speeds of more than thirty miles per hour. From tip to tip, the flukes of a great whale are longer than a tall person.

**VOCABULARY**
**horizontal flukes**—rounded, level parts.
**vertical**—perpendicular; straight up and down.
**spine**—backbone.

# stop+summarize

What does a whale use its tail for?

........................................................................................

........................................................................................

........................................................................................

........................................................................................

........................................................................................

Now return to the **L** column of your K-W-L Chart and record some of the information you learned.

## III. GATHER YOUR THOUGHTS

**A. CHOOSE A TOPIC** Plan to write an expository paragraph.

**1.** Write the names of 2 birds, 2 animals, and 2 insects.

**2.** Circle the one you know the most about.

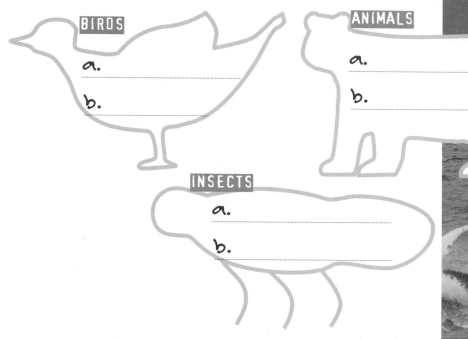

**BIRDS**

a.

b.

**ANIMALS**

a.

b.

**INSECTS**

a.

b.

**3.** What do you know about the one you circled? Write your thoughts or feelings about it below.

**B. WRITE A TOPIC SENTENCE** Now write a topic sentence for an expository paragraph. A topic sentence tells readers what the paragraph will be about. Use the formula to write your topic sentence.

**(a specific topic) + (a specific feeling or attitude) = a good topic sentence**

**EXAMPLE:** WHALES + (THEY ARE AMAZING) = WHALES ARE AMAZING ANIMALS.

_____ + _____
(your specific topic)          (your feeling or attitude)

= _____
(your topic sentence)

**C. GATHER DETAILS** The body of an expository paragraph gives details about the topic.

**1.** Write your topic sentence.

**2.** List 4 facts or characteristics that support your topic sentence.

**3.** Finish by writing a closing sentence that restates the main idea of your paragraph.

EXAMPLE:

These facts tell what is amazing about whales.

TOPIC SENTENCE: WHALES ARE AMAZING ANIMALS.

FACT #1 THEY ARE HUGE.

FACT #2 THEY ARE FAST.

FACT #3 THEY LIVE A LONG, LONG TIME.

FACT #4 THEY CAN STAY UNDERWATER FOR AN HOUR.

CLOSING SENTENCE: WHALES ARE THE MOST INCREDIBLE ANIMALS ON EARTH.

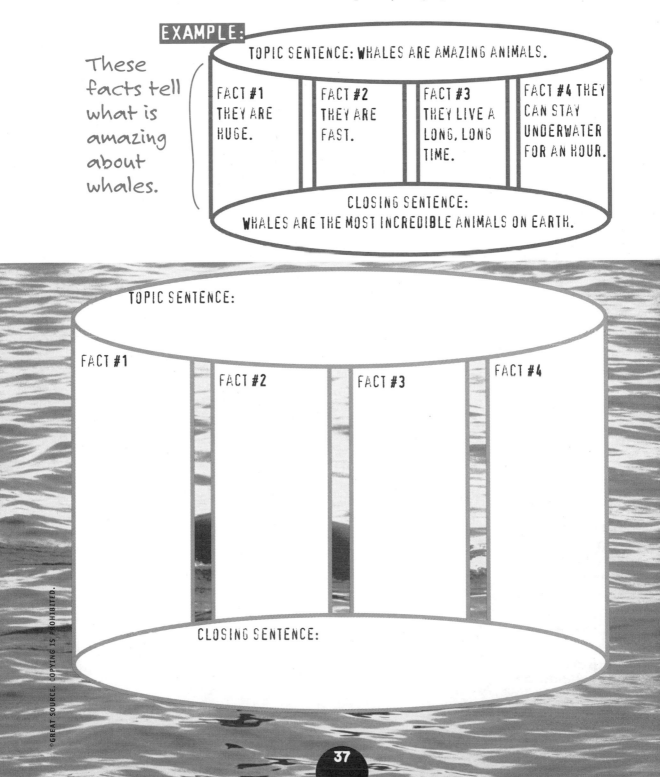

TOPIC SENTENCE:

FACT #1

FACT #2

FACT #3

FACT #4

CLOSING SENTENCE:

# IV. WRITE

Write an **expository paragraph** about the animal, bird, or insect you chose.

**1.** Begin with a topic sentence.

**2.** In the body of the paragraph, give 3 or 4 facts that support the topic sentence. End with a closing sentence.

**3.** Use the Writers' Checklist to help you revise.

# V. WRAP-UP
Did you find "The Great Whales" easy or hard to read? Why?

_____

_____

_____

_____

_____

_____

_____

_____

## 4: **Killer Whales**

Can you find out everything you need to know just by looking at something once? Of course you can't. We often appreciate things better the second, third, or even fourth time we see them.

## **BEFORE YOU READ**

Before you start to read, look through the selection quickly. Don't read every word. Instead, give the whole piece a "once over." This is called skimming.

**1.** First read the title and skim through the selection. Look for 4–5 key words and phrases that catch your eye.

**2.** Quickly read the first and last paragraphs.

**3.** When you've finished, answer the questions below.

## **Skimming Notes**

THIS SELECTION IS FICTION/NONFICTION BECAUSE:
(circle one)

○

WHAT 4–5 KEY WORDS AND PHRASES DID YOU NOTICE?

WHAT IS THE TOPIC OF THE FIRST PARAGRAPH?

○

WHAT IS THE LAST PARAGRAPH ABOUT?

## READ

Read "Killer Whales."

**1.** As you read, think about the main point the author is making.

**2.** Use the Response Notes to **clarify** at least 2 key details on each page of the selection.

**Response Notes**

### "Killer Whales" by Caroline Arnold

Killer whales are found in oceans all over the world, ranging from the icy waters near the <u>poles</u> to regions near the <u>equator</u>. They can be seen both in open water and along coastlines, but they are most common within 500 miles (806.5 kilometers) of land.

In the wild, killer whales live in groups called *pods*. The pod may have fewer than five or as many as twenty or more whales in it. The leader is one of the older females, and other members are her <u>offspring</u> or close relatives. A whale usually lives in its mother's pod for its whole life, and it develops strong ties with the other members.

In the wild, a pod may split into smaller groups, if it grows very large or if the leader dies. Each new pod consists of closely related whales and is led by one of the older females. Although the pods then hunt and travel separately, they may still meet occasionally and stay together for a short time. Groups of related pods are called *clans*.

EXAMPLE:
A whale's pod is like a family. A female leads the pod.

**VOCABULARY**

**poles**—either of the regions on the extremities of the earth's axis, the North Pole or South Pole.

**equator**—imaginary great circle around the earth's surface that divides the earth into the Northern Hemisphere and the Southern Hemisphere.

**offspring**—children.

**"Killer Whales"** continued

In the North Pacific, scientists have found that some groups of killer whales stay in the same general location all the time. They call these *resident pods*. Other groups, which they call <u>transient</u> pods, travel more widely. Resident pods, ranging from five to fifty killer whales, are usually larger than transient pods and are mainly fish eaters. Transient pods vary in size from one to seven animals and usually eat larger sea life, such as seals and other whales. Killer whales often hunt in groups. In this way, they can attack and kill creatures that are much larger than they are.

## stop+organize

| Key term | What is it? | What is it for? |
|---|---|---|
| pod | | |
| clan | | |
| resident pod | | |
| transient pod | | |

## stop+organize

Within each pod there is a social order. Scientists who study killer whales think that

**VOCABULARY**
*transient*—remaining in a place only a brief time.

such behavior as shoving, leaping out of the water, and splashing are some of the ways in which the whales <u>display</u> their strength and <u>assert</u> their <u>dominance</u>.

The <u>spectacular</u> leap out of the water that most whales do is a behavior called *breaching*. Breaching may be one way in which whales <u>communicate</u> with one another. Whales may also breach in order to knock off tiny animals called parasites that cling to their skin and <u>irritate</u> it. And it is possible that whales sometimes leap out of the water just for fun.

Because whales live in water, people sometimes think they are fish. They are not. Whales are mammals. Both fish and mammals need oxygen to live, but fish can get oxygen directly from the water. Whales cannot do this. They need to breathe air, just like mammals that live on land.

## stop+organize

| Key term | What is it? | What is it for? |
|----------|-------------|-----------------|
| breaching | | |
| mammal | | |

stop+organize

**VOCABULARY**
**display**—show.
**assert**—firmly express.
**dominance**—influence; control.
**spectacular**—amazing.
**communicate**—talk.
**irritate**—annoy.

**"Killer Whales"** continued

A whale breathes through a *blowhole*, an opening located on top of its head. At the blowhole, air goes into the nostrils, which are connected by the windpipe to the whale's lungs.

A whale rises to the surface of the water in order to breathe. First the whale blows a misty plume of air, called a *spout*, out of the blowhole. (A spout is formed by the condensation of moisture in the whale's warm breath when it is expelled into cooler air. It is like the tiny cloud your breath makes when you are outside on a frosty day.) After the whale exhales through the blowhole, it then takes a fresh breath of air. As the whale dives underwater, a special muscle closes the nostrils inside the blowhole so that water does not get in.

## stop+organize

| Key term | What is it? | What is it for? |
|----------|-------------|-----------------|
| spout    |             |                 |
| blowhole |             |                 |

stop+organize

**VOCABULARY**
**plume**—column.
**condensation**—process that makes liquid out of a gas.
**moisture**—wetness that may be felt.
**expelled**—forced out.
**exhales**—breathes out.

**"Killer Whales"** continued

Each species of whale has its own rate of breathing and a characteristic shape and direction of its spout. When killer whales are swimming on the surface, they breathe about twice a minute. When they dive, however, they usually stay underwater for four to five minutes before coming up for air. Occasionally they dive for as long as twelve minutes, and sometimes they have been known to stay underwater for as long as fifteen minutes.

During deep dives special adaptations help a whale to get along without breathing. Its heart slows down. Also, blood flow is reduced to parts of the body that can function without much oxygen. In this way more blood goes to the heart, lungs, and brain so they will continue to be supplied with the oxygen they need.

**VOCABULARY**
**species**—type.
**adaptations**—changes to suit the situation.
**supplied**—filled.

## stop+organize

**Word Bank**   Make a word bank to use when describing killer whales. Write a different word in each box.

| Killer Whales |
|---|

| breaching | mammal | | |
|---|---|---|---|
| | | | |
| | | | |

## GATHER YOUR THOUGHTS

**A. IDENTIFY THE MAIN IDEA** Get ready to write a summary paragraph about "Killer Whales."

**1.** First look back at the notes you wrote. Decide what main idea about killer whales the author is trying to communicate.

**2.** Complete the sentence below:

The main idea of "Killer Whales" is

**B. PLAN A SUMMARY.** Now build a summary of "Killer Whales."

**1.** Write the main idea.

**2.** Then look back at the reading. Find and list 4 details that support that idea.

**3.** Close with a final thought about what the author says about the whales.

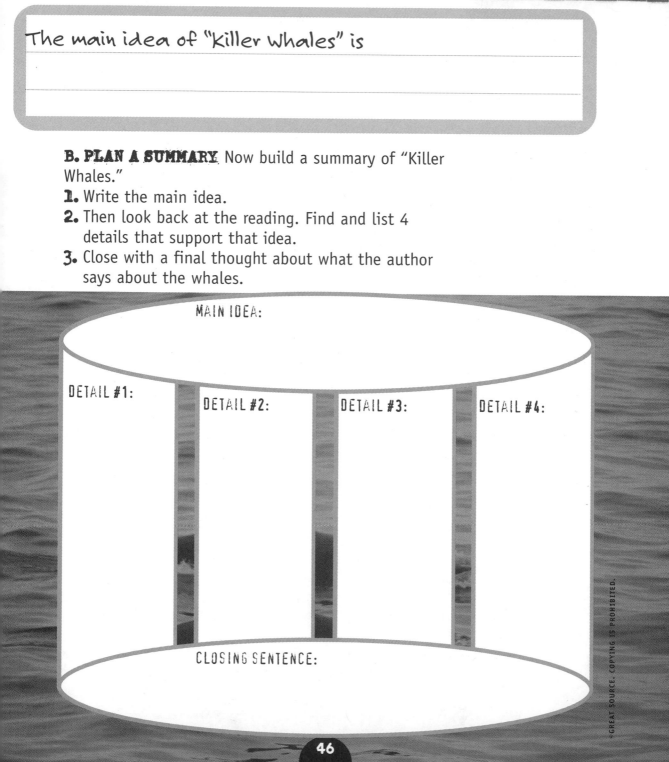

MAIN IDEA:

DETAIL #1:

DETAIL #2:

DETAIL #3:

DETAIL #4:

CLOSING SENTENCE:

©GREAT SOURCE. COPYING IS PROHIBITED.

# IV. WRITE

Write a **summary** of "Killer Whales."

**1.** State the main idea in the first sentence.

**2.** Support it with the 4 details from your organizer on page 46. Start a new sentence for each detail.

**3.** Use the Writers' Checklist when it is time to revise.

## WRITERS' CHECKLIST

### RUN-ONS

☐ Did you avoid writing run-on sentences? A run-on sentence is a compound sentence that is missing the comma and the conjunction. You can fix run-ons by inserting a comma and a conjunction or by breaking them into two separate sentences. EXAMPLES: *Whales are social creatures they live in pods.* (run-on) *Whales are social creatures, and they live in pods.* (correct) *Whales are social creatures. They live in pods.* (correct)

Continue your writing on the next page.

Continue your writing from the previous page.

_____

_____

_____

_____

_____

_____

_____

_____

## V. WRAP-UP

What did you like the most about "Killer Whales"?
Why?

**READERS' CHECKLIST**

**ENJOYMENT**
☐ Did you like the reading?
☐ Was the reading experience pleasurable?
☐ Would you want to reread the piece or recommend it to someone?

_____

_____

_____

_____

_____

_____

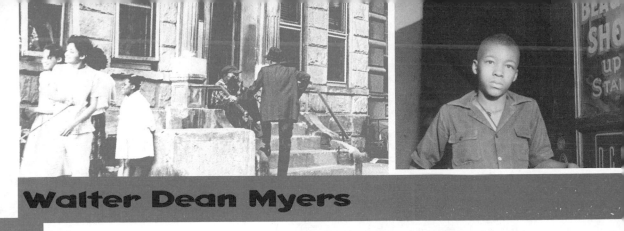

# Walter Dean Myers

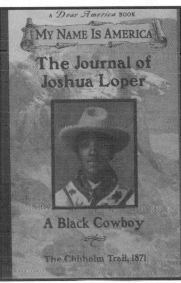

**W**alter Dean Myers was born in 1937 in West Virginia but grew up in Harlem, a neighborhood in New York City. Raised by foster parents, he had a happy but difficult childhood. In his autobiography "Bridges," Myers explains that his father could not read. But, as Myers writes, he told "absurdly wonderful stories" that "allowed me to release the balloon of my imagination."

A *Dear America* BOOK
MY NAME IS AMERICA
The Journal of
Joshua Loper
A Black Cowboy
The Chisholm Trail, 1871

Reading, writing, and talking—they all go together. Before you start reading, you can talk about the topic of the selection. As you read, you can "talk" to the writer and ask questions. When you've finished, you can talk and write what you think it was all about.

## BEFORE YOU READ

With a partner, take turns reading the sentences below from "Joshua."

**1.** Say what you think each sentence means.

**2.** Put a 1 before the sentence that you think comes first in the story, a 2 before the sentence that comes next, and so on. Share your answers with your reading partner.

**3.** Then predict what "Joshua" will be about.

**THINK–PAIR–SHARE**

| | |
|---|---|
| ☐ | "Mr. Muhlen called us all together in the afternoon. He said that it was important to him that the drive be successful." |
| ☐ | "'Mr. Muhlen wants you to go up north on the trail,' Mama said." |
| ☐ | "You went up the trail you were a man." |
| ☐ | "I did not look too excited, because I could see Mama was not too keen on the idea of me going on the trail." |
| ☐ | "I told him I was Joshua Loper and I was sixteen." |

## What do you think this story is about?

.......................................................................................

.......................................................................................

.......................................................................................

.......................................................................................

## II. READ

Now read "Joshua," which is an excerpt from an historical novel.

1. As you read, focus on the character of Joshua and how he is described.
2. Write in the Response Notes any **questions** you have about Joshua.

### "Joshua" from *The Journal of Joshua Loper* by Walter Dean Myers

**RESPONSE NOTES**

APRIL 30,1871

When I got home from church Mama wasn't home and there wasn't anything to eat, which was strange because Mama always made something special on Sundays. The weeds in our little <u>acre</u> needed pulling, but I knew I didn't want to get out in the sun with no hoe. I had been laying low since Captain Hunter came to the ranch. Mr. Muhlen had hired the Captain to run things since Charlie Taggert, our boss, bought himself a place up in Montana. I guess the Captain was a good man if Mr. Muhlen hired him, but he didn't seem to have any use for Colored folks and he didn't mind letting us know. When he first saw me I was sawing down boards to fix the porch on Mr. Muhlen's house. He asked me who I was and how old I was. I told him I was Joshua Loper and I was sixteen. He didn't say nothing, he just turned on his heel and walked away without another word.

I was still running the Captain through my mind when Mama got home. She had been

EXAMPLE:
How old is he?

**VOCABULARY**
**acre**—area of land.

over to Mr. Muhlen's house. Mama had worked for him all her life. Before the war he had been her master, but 'cause he liked her he let my father, Nehemiah, buy her freedom and marry up with her.

"Mr. Muhlen wants you to go up north on the trail," Mama said. "Guess you better go see him."

I did not look too excited, because I could see Mama was not too <u>keen</u> on the idea of me going on the trail. I went over to see Mr. Muhlen and he said it was true what Mama had said. He was real <u>short of hands</u> and he had to get together a <u>crew</u> to make the <u>drive to Abilene, Kansas</u>.

## STORY FRAME

### SETTING

**WHAT WAS THE TIME?**

**WHAT WAS THE PLACE?**

### CHARACTERS

**WHO ARE THE MAIN CHARACTERS?**

STORY FRAME

### VOCABULARY

**keen**—enthusiastic.
**short of hands**—in need of help.
**crew**—work group.
**drive to Abilene, Kansas**—In the 1880s, cattle were "driven" from ranches in Texas to be sold and shipped east by trains, which stopped in Abilene.

"When we going?" I asked.

"Got to get the <u>herd</u> up by mid July," Mr. Muhlen said. "Sooner the Captain gets them going the better."

I said I would do my best. Ain't nobody who went up the trail was talked about like they was a boy. You went up the trail you were a man.

MAY 1

Mr. Muhlen had an argument with Captain today. Captain said he did not want to take three Coloreds on the drive. Mr. Muhlen said he didn't have time to find another cook so he had to take Isaiah and he might as well take Doom and me, too.

"Joshua is a good boy," I heard Mr. Muhlen say. "He's done some quail hunting for me and his mama is a good, religious woman."

Captain didn't say nothing to me, but Jake Custis told me later I was still going. I told Timmy O'Hara and he said that I had better practice my running because the girls in Abilene was so fast they would run circles around me.

STORY FRAME

PLOT OR CONFLICT

WHAT IS THE PROBLEM OR CHALLENGE IN THE STORY?

WHICH CHARACTER WILL FACE THIS CHALLENGE OR PROBLEM?

VOCABULARY
**herd**—group of cattle.

STORY FRAME

Timmy was my best friend on the Slash M Ranch and I knew he would help me out on the drive. When he asked me if I was glad I was going, I said it was okay.

"If it's just okay," he said, "how come you grinning so much?"

Timmy was seventeen, a year older than me, and he had made his first trail drive at sixteen, the same age I was. He wasn't what you would call a good-looking fellow, but he had a look about him that made you think that any minute he was going to bust out into a smile. His eyes were kind of gray if you looked at them straight on and kind of green if you looked at them from the side. He said that was from his being Irish. There wasn't any question about him being one of the top hands even though he was young. He could get the job done and no matter what he had to chew on he never spit out a bad word about anybody. I didn't say anything to him about the Captain not wanting to take the Coloreds on the drive.

Mr. Muhlen called us all together in the afternoon. He said that it was important to him that the drive be successful.

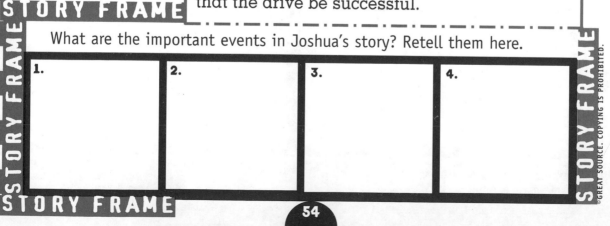

## STORY FRAME

What are the important events in Joshua's story? Retell them here.

| 1. | 2. | 3. | 4. |
|----|----|----|----|
|    |    |    |    |

STORY FRAME

## GATHER YOUR THOUGHTS

**A. DESCRIBE A CHARACTER** On the web below, write 8 or more words that describe Joshua.

How he feels

How he looks

$$\boxed{\text{Joshua}}$$

What he says

How he acts

**B. DEVELOP A TOPIC SENTENCE** Get ready to write a character sketch of Joshua.

**1.** Use 2 words you wrote above to complete the topic sentence.

| MY TOPIC SENTENCE |
| --- |
| Joshua Loper is both |
| and |

**2.** Next look back at the reading. List 2 details from the story to support each word.

| JOSHUA IS | |
| --- | --- |
| DETAIL #1 | |
| DETAIL #2 | |

| AND | |
| --- | --- |
| DETAIL #1 | |
| DETAIL #2 | |

# IV. WRITE

Write a **character sketch** of Joshua Loper.

1. Start with your topic sentence.
2. Then give details about his character.
3. Finish with a closing sentence that says how you feel about him.
4. Use the Writers' Checklist to help you revise.

## V. WRAP-UP

What are some of the things that "Joshua" made you think about?

_____

_____

_____

_____

_____

_____

_____

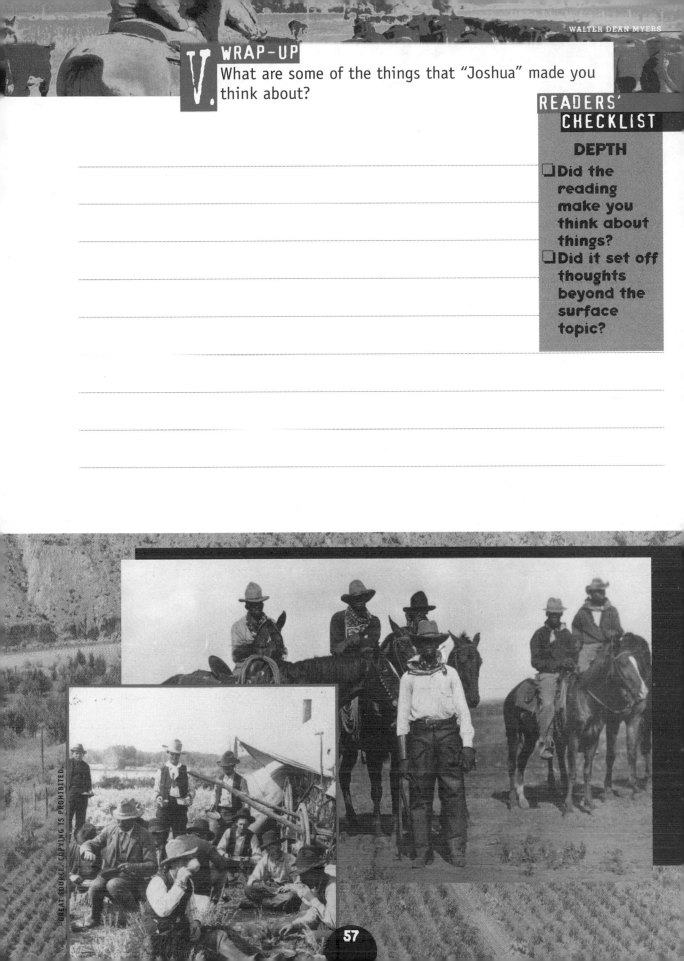

# 6: The Man

Some places can make an impression on you almost as soon as you get there. They seem fun or serious or spooky or inviting. A story can make an impression on you, too. The impression you get from a story is called the *mood*.

**BEFORE YOU READ**

Glance quickly through "The Man."
1. Then read the words in the Story Impression below.
2. Write a sentence for each word on the left, telling what you think this story is about.

## STORY IMPRESSION

| Jimmy | |
| --- | --- |
| money | |
| father's name | |
| jail | |
| Mama Jean | |
| photo album | |
| fifteen | |

## II. READ

Now carefully read this excerpt from Walter Dean Myers's novel.

**1.** As you read, think about the mood of the story.

**2. Mark** or **highlight** details that interest you and write about them in the Response Notes.

**"The Man"** from *Somewhere in the Darkness* by Walter Dean Myers

The man was tall and so thin that Jimmy could see the outline of his shoulder bones through the dark green shirt he wore. He had an odd way of holding his head down and looking up at Jimmy. Jimmy opened his mouth so that the man in front of him couldn't tell how quickly he was breathing. He moved the key away from the mailbox.

"I know you don't remember me," the man said. His voice was flat and low so that Jimmy had to <u>strain</u> to hear him.

"How you doing?" Jimmy asked. The words came out higher than he wanted them to.

EXAMPLE:
His voice seems
scary.

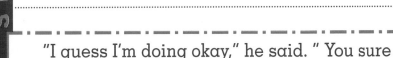

**STOP**

Who do you think the man is?

..................................................

..................................................

**STOP AND PREDICT**

"I guess I'm doing okay," he said. " You sure got big."

"What's my name?" Jimmy asked.

"Your name is Jimmy."

" It's really James," Jimmy said.

"No, it's not," the man said. "It's Jimmy, because that was your mother's brother's

**VOCABULARY**
**strain** try very hard.

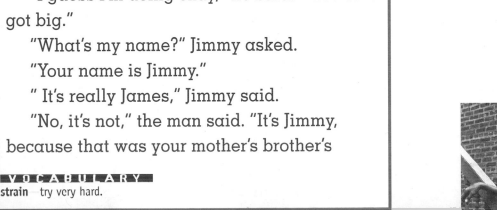

name. That's who you named after."

"I thought . . ." Jimmy searched for the words. "Mama Jean said you were . . . away."

"I'm out now," the man said.

"You want to go upstairs?"

The man smiled. "How I know you really my boy?" he said. "You might be some kind of stick-up man who gets people in their apartment and then takes their money."

"You the one that said you were my father," Jimmy said.

"You remember my name?"

"What is it?"

"It's really Cephus, but that ain't what they call me."

"Crab?"

## STOP AND PREDICT

What will Jimmy do next?

.................................................................................................

.................................................................................................

## STOP AND PREDICT

The man nodded, and Jimmy thought that there, in the light slanting down from the window, he saw a glistening in the man's eyes before he turned away. In a moment he had turned back toward Jimmy. " I guess we can go up and sit down for a while."

Jimmy wasn't sure. The man knew his father's name, even what people called him, but he didn't look like the picture in Mama Jean's album. He was skinny, he could have been a crack head.

**VOCABULARY**
**glistening**—sparkling.

**"The Man"** continued

"You scared to let me inside," the man said, leaning against the <u>banister</u>. "It's okay. We can wait for Jean to come home."

STOP AND PREDICT

**What do you think the man wants?**

Jimmy went up the stairs first. He didn't know what to think. In a way he was afraid, but he wasn't sure why. Mama Jean had told him that his father was in jail. She hadn't said anything about him coming out any time soon. When they reached the apartment Jimmy thought about what he would do if the man wasn't his father and tried to do something. He walked funny; Jimmy thought he could probably outrun the guy.

He unlocked the door and opened it. The man walked away, and for a moment Jimmy thought he was leaving, but then he picked up a jacket and a package from the stairs that Jimmy hadn't noticed before and came back to the door.

"You were up here before?" Jimmy asked.

"A while ago," the man said.

Jimmy stood aside and let him in. He walked in and looked around and nodded <u>approvingly</u>.

"When you get out?"

"Last week," the man said. "Took me a

**VOCABULARY**
**banister**—handrail of a staircase.
**approvingly**—in favor.

while to figure out what I wanted to do. Got any coffee or anything?"

"I can make some, " Jimmy said. "I got to put my books away first."

"Yeah, okay." The man sat down on a kitchen chair next to the table and stretched his legs out in front of him.

Jimmy went into Mama Jean's bedroom, looked under the Bible stand, and found her photo album. He turned the pages as quickly as he could, past the picture in the soldier's uniform because it was too dark, then found the one he was looking for.

In the picture was a tall, well-built man leaning against a car. There was a woman standing next to him and next to the woman was Mama Jean. The woman in between was his mother.

The man in the picture didn't look much like the man in the other room except for the wide forehead and the way he was tilting his head forward and looking up out of the picture.

STOP AND PREDICT

What do you predict Jimmy will do now?

................................................................................

................................................................................

STOP AND PREDICT

"It look like me?"

Jimmy jumped and slammed the book shut.

"Let's see it," the man said.

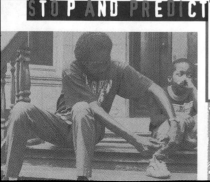

**"The Man"** continued

Jimmy looked through the book again, slowly, until he found the picture. Then he showed it to the man.

"Me and your mama were thinking about buying a car," the man said, holding up the album. "We went up to the Bronx and looked at some and figured out how much we were going to need for a <u>down payment</u>. We were talking about getting it up, I think it was a hundred dollars, something like that. It wasn't real talk because we didn't have no hundred dollars to be putting out. Dolly told Jean and Jean said maybe we could all buy a car together. Jean and your mama were tight, real tight."

"You buy the car?"

"No, we got our piece of the money together and then your mama wanted to buy a living room set and that was that. You know how a woman can get with that kind of thing."

Jimmy looked at the picture again, then went into the kitchen.

He found the pot and started spooning coffee into the basket.

"How come you didn't write and let everybody know you were coming?" he asked as he ran tap water into the pot.

"Didn't know what I wanted to do," Crab said. He took out a <u>handkerchief</u>, coughed into it, and then spit into it.

"There's some Kleenex on the counter," Jimmy said.

**VOCABULARY**
**down payment**—partial payment made at the time something is bought, with the other part to be paid later.
**handkerchief**—small piece of cloth used for wiping the nose or mouth.

"I didn't think you were going to be so big," Crab said. "You know, I had this thing in my head that I was going see you and pick you up and put you on top of the refrigerator. You imagine me trying to pick you up and put you on the refrigerator?"

"Put me on what . . . ?" Even as he said the words an image came to him, of him looking down from the refrigerator and reaching for somebody.

"I used to do that when you were a kid," the man said.

"Oh."

"How you doing in school and everything?"

"Okay." Jimmy finished putting the water in the coffeepot and put it on the stove. He looked over at the man and saw him watching him. "Sometimes I make coffee for Mama Jean," he said.

"You fourteen, now?"

"Almost fifteen," Jimmy said. "In a couple of months."

"Yeah, okay."

"So now you decided what you going to do?" Jimmy turned down the flame until it was an even glow under the <u>battered</u> aluminum pot.

"Yeah," the man said. "I thought you and me might go around the country a bit."

A knock came on the door, and the man froze for a moment, then held his hand up to Jimmy. "I want to surprise Jean," he said.

**VOCABULARY**
battered—beat up.

# GATHER YOUR THOUGHTS

**A. QUICKWRITE** In the story, Jimmy had not seen his father for a long time. Get ready to write a letter to someone you haven't seen for a long time.

1. Choose a person. To find some things to say, do a 1-minute quickwrite.
2. In the quickwrite, list anything about you that comes to mind.

**1-MINUTE QUICKWRITE**

**B. SORT IDEAS** Review what you wrote.
1. Then ask yourself, "What might the person I write to want to know about me?"
2. Choose and write 2 ideas to include in your letter.

EXAMPLE
idea #1: What I've been doing at school
idea #2: My hobbies and interests

idea #1

idea #2

# WRITE

Write a **letter** to a person you haven't seen for a long time.
1. Write about 2 main ideas.
2. Start a new paragraph for each new idea.
3. Use the Writers' Checklist to help you revise.

_____ (date)

(opening) _____

..................................................

..................................................

## WRITERS' CHECKLIST

### LETTERS

☐ Did you capitalize each word in the opening and remember to put a comma after the last word of the opening?
EXAMPLE: _Dear Ashley,_

☐ Did you capitalize only the first word in the closing and use a comma at the end? EXAMPLE:
_Sincerely yours,_

..................................................

..................................................

..................................................

..................................................

(closing) _____

..................................................

# V. WRAP-UP

What did you like most about Walter Dean Myers's writing style? What did you like least?

## READERS' CHECKLIST

### STYLE

☐ Did you find the passage well written?

☐ Does the style show you how to be a better writer?

..................................................

..................................................

..................................................

rest eighth inch.

$$\frac{3}{4}$$

$$\frac{5}{8}$$

# Decisions

Decisions

$$\frac{1}{8} \text{ inch}$$

1

**S**ometimes you only have one chance to make the right decision. That's why it's important to consider the consequences. Think about how your choices will affect yourself and others. Then make your decision and live with it.

the nearest eighth inc

timate:

$= 2\ell +$

$= (2 \times 2$

$= (2 \times \frac{1}{8}$

$= \frac{38}{8} +$

$\frac{38}{}$

# What Happened During the Ice Storm

**Do you like surprises?** Most people do. When you're reading, it's fun to guess what might happen next. A picture walk can help you make predictions about a story or article.

## I. BEFORE YOU READ

Do a picture walk. Page through "What Happened During the Ice Storm."

**1.** Look carefully at every picture and read each caption.

**2.** Then complete the sentences below with a partner.

## Picture Walk

These pictures make me feel . . .

The pictures remind me of . . .

I predict this story will be about . . .

I have these questions about the pictures:

## READ

Now read the story by Jim Heynen.
1. As you are reading, **predict** how you think things will turn out.
2. Write your predictions in the Response Notes.

### "What Happened During the Ice Storm"
### by Jim Heynen

One winter there was a freezing rain. How beautiful! people said when things outside started to shine with ice. But the freezing rain kept coming. Tree branches glistened like glass. Then broke like glass. Ice thickened on the windows until everything outside blurred. Farmers moved their livestock into the barns, and most animals were safe. But not the pheasants. Their eyes froze shut.

Some farmers went ice-skating down the gravel roads with clubs to harvest the pheasants that sat helplessly in the roadside ditches. The boys went out into the freezing rain to find pheasants too. They saw dark spots along a fence. Pheasants, all right. Five or six of them. The boys slid their feet along slowly, trying not to break the ice that covered the snow. They slid up close to the pheasants. The pheasants pulled their heads down between their wings. They couldn't tell how easy it was to see them huddled there.

EXAMPLE:

The pheasants will die from the ice storm.

**VOCABULARY**
**glistened**—sparkled.
**livestock**—farm animals.
**pheasants**—birds with long tails.
**harvest**—gather.
**huddled**—standing close together.

**Two pheasants**

## Double-entry Journal

First, look at the example. Then read the quote from the story in the left-hand column. Write your own thoughts about it.

| Quote | My thoughts |
|---|---|
| EXAMPLE:<br>"Tree branches glistened like glass. Then broke like glass." | Breaking glass sounds loud. |
| "Some farmers went ice-skating down the gravel roads with clubs to harvest the pheasants that sat helplessly in the roadside ditches." | |

**Response Notes**

A young man and his dog riding through an ice storm

**"What Happened During the Ice Storm"** continued

The boys stood still in the icy rain. Their breath came out in slow puffs of steam. The pheasants' breath came out in quick little white puffs. Some of them lifted their heads and turned them from side to side, but they were blindfolded with ice and didn't <u>flush</u>. The boys had not brought clubs, or sacks, or anything but themselves. They stood over the pheasants, turning their own heads, looking at each other, each expecting the other to do something. To <u>pounce</u> on a pheasant, or to yell Bang! Things around them were shining and dripping with icy rain. The barbed-wire fence. The fence posts. The broken stems of grass. Even the grass seeds. The grass seeds looked like little yolks inside <u>gelatin</u> whites. And the pheasants looked like unborn birds <u>glazed</u> in egg white. Ice was hardening on the boys' caps and coats. Soon they would be covered with ice too.

**VOCABULARY**
**flush**—fly off from a hiding spot.
**pounce**—leap or swoop.
**gelatin**—jellylike.
**glazed**—covered with a shiny substance.

**70**

## Double-entry Journal

Respond to the quote.

| Quote | My thoughts |
|---|---|
| "They stood over the pheasants, turning their own heads, looking at each other, each expecting the other to do something." | |

**"What Happened During the Ice Storm"** continued

Then one of the boys said, Shh. He was taking off his coat, the thin layer of ice splintering in flakes as he pulled his arms from the sleeves. But the inside of the coat was dry and warm. He covered two of the <u>crouching</u> pheasants with his coat, rounding the back of it over them like a shell. The other boys did the same. They covered all the helpless pheasants. The small gray hens and the larger brown cocks. Now the boys felt the rain soaking through their shirts and freezing. They ran across the slippery fields, unsure of their footing, the ice clinging to their skin as they made their way toward the blurry lights of the house.

**VOCABULARY**
**crouching**—bending low.

## Double-entry Journal

Write your ideas and feelings about the quote.

| Quote | My thoughts |
|---|---|
| "Now the boys felt the rain soaking through their shirts and freezing." | |

**A. REFLECT** Think about the story. Why do the boys help the pheasants? What prompted their kindness?

**B. RECALL AN EXPERIENCE** Think about different times you've performed an act of kindness.
**1.** Tell about one act of kindness in the frames below.
**2.** Try to fill in every frame.

## ACT OF KINDNESS

## WHO WAS THERE?

## WHEN DID IT HAPPEN?

## WHAT EXACTLY HAPPENED?

## WHERE WERE YOU?

## WHY DID YOU DO IT?

## HOW DID YOU FEEL AFTERWARD?

# IV. WRITE

Write a **journal entry** about a time you were kind.

1. Begin by explaining what the act of kindness was, who was there, and when it took place.
2. Then explain what happened. In the last sentence, tell how you felt about doing it.
3. Use the Writers' Checklist to help you revise, even though this is only a journal entry.

Continue your writing on the next page.

## WRITERS' CHECKLIST

### CAPITALIZATION

☐ Did you capitalize the names of particular persons, places, and things?
EXAMPLE: *My brother Andy won a trip to Orlando, Florida.*

☐ Did you capitalize the names of days of the week and months? EXAMPLE: *The first Monday in January was a lucky day.*

☐ Did you capitalize the pronoun I?
EXAMPLE: *Katie and I found the money last week.*

Continue your writing from the previous page.

## V. WRAP-UP

What did you learn from reading "What Happened During the Ice Storm"?

**READERS' CHECKLIST**

**MEANING**

- ❑ Did you learn something from the reading?
- ❑ Did it affect you or make an impression?

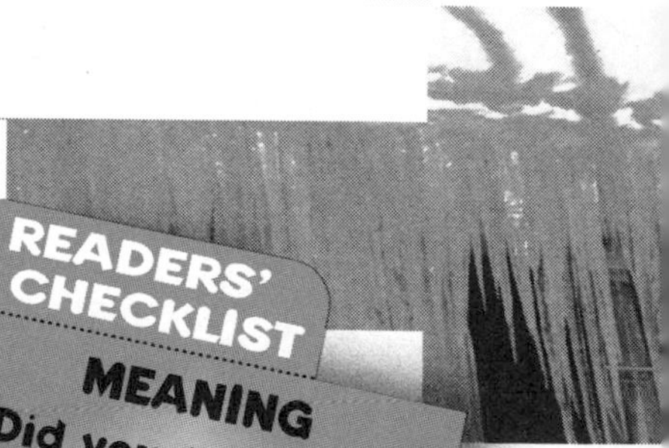

# 8: Cheating

Have you ever done something that you know is wrong, but you just couldn't help yourself? The boy in the next story has this problem. Think about how his problem connects to something in your own life.

## I. BEFORE YOU READ

To get a feeling for a subject, think about your own opinions of it.

**1.** Read each statement and mark whether you agree or disagree.

**2.** Then make a prediction about the story.

## Anticipation Guide

| BEFORE YOU READ | | | AFTER YOU READ | |
|---|---|---|---|---|
| agree | disagree | | agree | disagree |
| ⬭ | ⬭ | Everyone cheats. | ⬭ | ⬭ |
| ⬭ | ⬭ | Sometimes cheating is OK. | ⬭ | ⬭ |
| ⬭ | ⬭ | Cheaters are bad to the core. | ⬭ | ⬭ |
| ⬭ | ⬭ | Parents should always punish kids for cheating. | ⬭ | ⬭ |
| ⬭ | ⬭ | Cheaters should sometimes go to jail. | ⬭ | ⬭ |
| ⬭ | ⬭ | I'd rather fail a test than cheat on it. | ⬭ | ⬭ |

What do you think will happen in this story?

......................................................................................

......................................................................................

......................................................................................

## II.  READ
Read the selection slowly and carefully.
**1.** As you read, think about how you would react in a similar situation.
**2.** Write your own **reactions** and comments in the Response Notes.

**Response Notes**

### "Cheating" from *Family Secrets*
### by Susan Shreve

The fact is, I couldn't believe what I'd done <u>in cold blood</u>. I began to wonder about myself—really wonder—things like whether I would steal from stores or hurt someone on purpose or do some other terrible thing I couldn't even imagine. I began to wonder whether I was plain bad to the core.

I've never been a wonderful kid that everybody in the world loves and thinks is swell, like Nicho. I have a bad temper and I like to have my own way and I argue a lot. Sometimes I can be mean. But most of the time I've thought of myself as a pretty <u>decent</u> kid. Mostly I work hard, I stick up for little kids, and I tell the truth. Mostly I like myself fine—except I wish I were better at basketball.

Now all of a sudden I've turned into this criminal. It's hard to believe I'm just a boy. And all because of one stupid math test.

**EXAMPLE:**
I think the same thing about myself.

**VOCABULARY**
**in cold blood**—on purpose and without feeling.
**decent**—good.

Lying on the floor of my room, I begin to think that probably I've been bad all along. It just took this math test to <u>clinch</u> it. I'll probably never tell the truth again.

**Story Frame**

THIS STORY ----▶
TAKES PLACE

                    ·········▶ IS TELLING THE
                              STORY.

                              A PROBLEM
                              HAPPENS WHEN ·······▶

I tell my mother I'm sick when she calls me to come down for dinner. She doesn't believe me, but puts me to bed anyhow. I lie there in the early winter darkness wondering what terrible thing I'll be doing next when my father comes in and sits down on my bed.

"What's the matter?" he asks.

"I've got a stomachache," I say. Luckily, it's too dark to see his face.

"Is that all?"

"Yeah."

"Mommy says you've been in your room since school."

"I was sick there, too," I say.

"She thinks something happened today and you're upset."

That's the thing that really drives me crazy about my mother. She knows things sitting inside my head same as if I was turned inside out.

**VOCABULARY**
**clinch**—prove; make sure of.

**"Cheating"** continued

"Well," my father says. I can tell he doesn't believe me.

"My stomach is feeling sort of upset." I <u>hedge</u>.

"Okay," he says and he pats my leg and gets up.

Just as he shuts the door to my room I call out to him in a voice I don't even recognize as my own that I'm going to have to run away.

"How come?" he calls back not surprised or anything.

So I tell him I cheated on this math test. To tell the truth, I'm pretty much surprised at myself. I didn't plan to tell him anything.

## Story Frame

AFTER THE PROBLEM DEVELOPS, WHAT HAPPENS NEXT IS

↓

He doesn't say anything at first and that just about kills me. I'd be fine if he'd spank me or something. To say nothing can drive a person crazy.

And then he says I'll have to call Mr. Burke. It's not what *I* had in mind.

"Now?" I ask, surprised.

"Now," he says. He turns on the light and pulls off my covers.

"I'm not going to," I say.

But I do it. I call Mr. Burke, probably waking him up, and I tell him exactly what happened,

**VOCABULARY**

**hedge**—say unconvincingly.

even that I decided to cheat the night before the test. He says I'll come in Saturday to take another test, which is okay with me, and I thank him a whole lot for being understanding and all. He's not friendly but he's not <u>absolutely</u> mean either.

**Story Frame**

THE INCIDENT ENDS WHEN

"Today I thought I was turning into a criminal," I tell my father when he turns out my light.

Sometimes my father kisses me good night and sometimes he doesn't. I never know. But tonight he does.

**VOCABULARY**
**absolutely**—completely.

**Story Frame**

WHAT IS THE AUTHOR'S MAIN IDEA OR MESSAGE IN THE STORY?

Return to the Anticipation Guide on page 75 and fill in the "After You Read" column.

A $4\frac{3}{8}$ inches
B 7 inches
C 10 inche
D 11.2 i

7 in.

M

5 in.

N

x in.

P

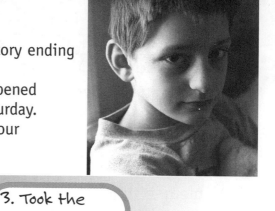

## III. GATHER YOUR THOUGHTS

**CREATE A PLOT** Get ready to write a new story ending for "Cheating."

**1.** Create an episode that explains what happened during the meeting with Mr. Burke on Saturday.

**2.** Complete the storyboards below to plan your ending.

EXAMPLE

| 1. Apologized to Mr. Burke. | 2. Mr. Burke told a story. | 3. Took the test, and left. |

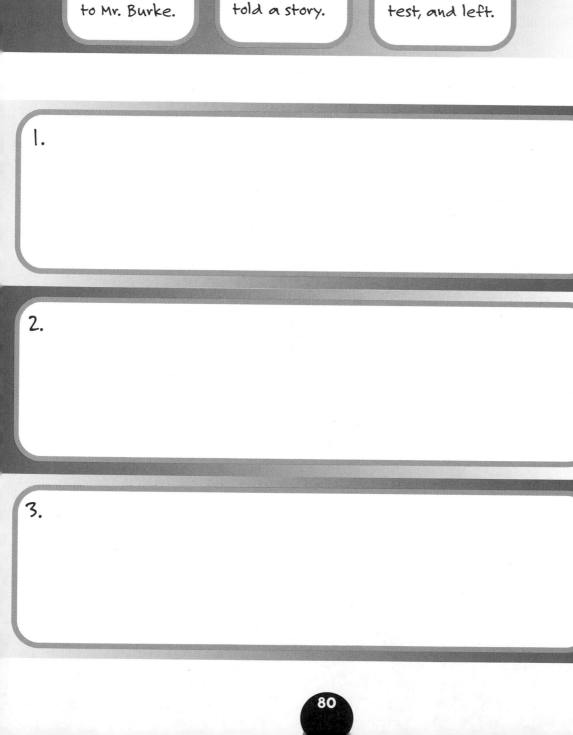

1.

2.

3.

# IV. WRITE

Write a new **story ending** for "Cheating."

**1.** Use your notes from page 80. Begin your story with Mr. Burke's first words during the Saturday meeting.

**2.** Use the Writers' Checklist to help you revise.

Continue your writing on the next page.

## WRITERS' CHECKLIST

### DIALOGUE

❏ Did you use quotation marks at the beginning and end of each quotation? EXAMPLE: "I'm here to take my test," I said.

❏ Did you use commas to separate quotations from speech tags? EXAMPLE: "Take a seat, then," Mr. Burke replied.

❏ Did you check to see that the quotation itself contains the correct punctuation? EXAMPLE: "Where?" I asked.

Continue your writing from the previous page.

_____

_____

_____

_____

_____

_____

_____

_____

_____

## V. WRAP-UP

What was your favorite part of "Cheating"? Why?

_____

_____

_____

_____

_____

_____

**READERS' CHECKLIST**

**ENJOYMENT**

☐ Did you like the reading?

☐ Was the reading experience pleasurable?

☐ Would you want to reread the piece or recommend it to someone?

# Civilizations

Our knowledge of history and culture has a great deal to do with the study of ancient civilizations. The discovery of mummies from Egyptian and South American civilizations has helped researchers to understand what life was like thousands of years ago.

Sometimes you can tell a lot about a person even if you only get a quick glimpse. The same is true for reading. A quick glance at a text can give you a lot of information: what it's about, where it takes place, and who's involved.

## I. BEFORE YOU READ

Preview "Egyptian Mummies."

1. Read the first and the last paragraphs.
2. Underline the 2 most important words in each line of these paragraphs.
3. Then answer the questions below.

## PREVIEW CARD

### WHAT IS THE SELECTION ABOUT?

### WHAT IS THE TIME PERIOD?

### WHAT QUESTIONS DO YOU HAVE FOR THE AUTHOR?

# READ

Now read the rest of "Egyptian Mummies."

**1.** As you read, pay attention to how the mummies are described.

**2. Clarify** important details in the Response Notes.

### "Egyptian Mummies" by Charlotte Wilcox

Egyptian mummies have been the subject of <u>legends</u> for thousands of years. It was once believed that ancient Egyptians used secret spells to <u>preserve</u> bodies. No Egyptian writings have ever been found telling exactly how Egyptians made mummies. But a Greek writer, Herodotus, visited Egypt over 2,000 years ago and saw mummies being <u>embalmed</u>. Thanks to Herodotus and to modern research, the process the Egyptians used is no longer a mystery.

The oldest Egyptian mummies, from before 2500 BC, were not embalmed at all. They became mummies naturally.

EXAMPLE:
Not all mummies
were embalmed.

STOP AND THINK

How long ago did the Egyptians start making mummies?

........................................................................

........................................................................

........................................................................

STOP AND THINK

#### VOCABULARY
**legends**—ancient stories.
**preserve**—protect; maintain.
**embalmed**—covered or filled with a substance to prevent rotting.

In early times, bodies were simply wrapped in cloth or leather and buried in the sand. Warm desert winds and hot sun heating the sand caused bodies to dry out very quickly, so they did not <u>decay</u>.

Even very early in their history, Egyptians believed in life after death. Pottery and jewelry were put in graves for the dead to use. Over time, this belief grew into a religion. As the Egyptian religion grew, so did the importance of taking care of the dead.

**STOP AND THINK**

Why did the Egyptians bury pottery and jewelry along with their dead?

.............................................................................

.............................................................................

.............................................................................

Egyptian kings, called pharaohs, were thought to be gods. When a pharaoh died, Egyptians thought his spirit turned into Osiris, god-king of the dead. The dead pharaoh's son became ruler of Egypt in his place. Egyptians called their ruler Horus, god-king of the living.

**VOCABULARY**
decay—rot.

In order for the pharaoh's spirit to live in the spirit world, Egyptians thought it had to have a body to rest in on earth. They thought that if the body looked something like the pharaoh did when he was alive, his spirit would recognize it.

During his life, a pharaoh made <u>lavish</u> preparations for the life he expected to live after death. He stored food, clothing, books, medicine, gold and jewels, weapons, furniture, and other things he enjoyed in life.

Egyptians believed that the spirits of the dead needed their own houses. At first this was done by building underground rooms, called tombs, where the body and other things were buried.

Later pharaohs built rooms or houses over the tombs. As each pharaoh tried to outdo the ones before, the houses became larger and more beautiful.

The largest of all the tomb houses were the pyramids.

**VOCABULARY**
**lavish**—overly fancy.

**What were tombs and pyramids used for?**

**RESPONSE NOTES**    **"Egyptian Mummies"** continued

Over 70 pharaohs built pyramids for themselves. The Great Pyramid, built by Pharaoh Khufu over 4,000 years ago, is still the largest stone structure in the world. Until about a hundred years ago, it was also the world's tallest building.

# III. GATHER YOUR THOUGHTS

**A. ORGANIZE INFORMATION** What did you learn about Egyptian mummies? Show what you know on this web.

HOW WERE THEY MADE?

WHAT WAS MOST INTERESTING TO YOU?

Egyptian Mummies

WHEN WERE THEY MADE?

WHY WERE THEY MADE?

**B. GATHER DETAILS** Get ready to write a descriptive paragraph about Egyptian mummies.
1. First make a word bank of words you might use when talking about them.
2. Try to list at least 10 words about Egyptian mummies.

| tombs | pharaoh | | |
|-------|---------|--|--|
|  |  |  |  |
|  |  |  |  |
|  |  |  |  |

**WORD BANK**

**C. WRITE A TOPIC SENTENCE** Now draft a topic sentence for a descriptive paragraph about mummies.

## WRITE

Write a **descriptive paragraph** about mummies.

**1.** Start with a topic sentence.

**2.** Then give details that can help your readers "see" what you are describing.

**3.** Use the Writers' Checklist when you revise.

## WRITERS' CHECKLIST

### VERB PAIRS

☐ Did you use *bring* and *take* correctly? *Bring* is a verb that means "to carry with" and is used when something is carried toward the speaker. *Take* is a verb that means to "capture or take hold of" and is used when something is carried away from the speaker.

EXAMPLES: *Pharaohs would bring jewels with them. People would take bodies away for burial.*

☐ Did you use *let* and *leave* correctly? *Let* means "not to stop something from happening." *Leave* means "to go away" or "not to take away."

EXAMPLES: *They would leave pots in the graves. To let a spirit live, Egyptians created mummies.*

## V. WRAP-UP

What is "Egyptian Mummies" about?

### READERS' CHECKLIST

**UNDERSTANDING**

☐ Did you understand the reading?

☐ Was the message or point clear?

☐ Can you restate what the reading is about?

Good readers are never empty-handed. They always bring everything they know about the topic with them. Organizers such as K-W-L charts can help you keep track of what you already know and what you want to find out.

## BEFORE YOU READ

Complete the K-W-L Chart below.

1. Write what you know about mummies in the **K** space.

2. Write what you want to learn in the **W** space. Save the **L** space for later.

### K-W-L CHART

**WHAT I KNOW**

K

**WHAT I WANT TO KNOW**

W

**WHAT I LEARNED**

L

## READ

Now read this selection from *Tales Mummies Tell*.
**1.** As you read, pay special attention to information about different kinds of mummies.
**2.** Write **questions** you have in the Response Notes.

---

### "Mummies" by Patricia Lauber

The word *mummies* usually makes people think of ancient Egyptians wrapped in bands of linen. Egyptian mummies are the most famous, but they are far from being the only ones. Peoples in many parts of the world have made mummies of their dead, and a great many other mummies have formed naturally. . . .

Most mummies, whether natural or manmade, formed by <u>rapid</u> drying. Ordinarily, when a living thing dies, <u>decay</u> soon sets in. The decay is caused by bacteria, molds, and other small forms of life. As they feed on dead material, they break it down. The material, which is rich in minerals that plants need, is added to the soil. In this way the material is <u>recycled</u>. It is used by plants, which are eaten by animals. To do their work, bacteria and other small living things need water. They

**VOCABULARY**
**rapid**—fast.
**decay**—rotting.
**recycled**—used again.

**RESPONSE NOTES**

EXAMPLE:
Where else besides Egypt were mummies made?

cannot <u>multiply</u> or grow without it. If dead material dries out rapidly and stays dry, decay does not take place. In fact, for thousands of years people have been <u>preserving</u> meat and fish this way, by drying them in the sun or packing them in salt, which draws water from the tissues.

Mummies have often formed naturally in deserts, where hot dry sands rapidly drew water out of the body tissues. Probably the first Egyptian mummies were made by accident in this way, when early settlers of the Nile Valley buried their dead in the desert, outside the <u>fertile</u> farmland.

Others have formed in similar ways. Copper Man is a South American mummy that formed naturally with the help of dry air and salts. This mummy was once a copper miner who lived and worked around A.D. 800 in the Atacama Desert of northern Chile. He was in a mine, hammering rock and <u>prying</u> out copper <u>ore</u>, when the tunnel in which he was working <u>collapsed</u> and killed him. His mummy was found in 1899, with its arms still out in a working position. His hair was neatly braided and he wore a <u>loincloth</u>. Near him were the

**VOCABULARY**
**multiply**—increase in number.
**preserving**—keeping fresh.
**fertile**—good for growing plants.
**prying**—digging.
**ore**—valuable substance mined from a rock.
**collapsed**—fell down; caved in.
**loincloth**—short cloth covering the hip area.

**Mummy of an Atacama Indian, discovered in Chile, in a crouched position and wearing long braids**

**"Mummies"** continued

tools of his <u>trade</u>: four <u>coiled</u> baskets for <u>hauling</u> out rock; a <u>rawhide</u> bag for ore; a stone hammer; a spade-shaped stone too. He was named Copper Man because the copper salts that helped preserve his body combined with oxygen had <u>stained</u> his body a dull green.

STOP AND RECORD

Record information you want to remember about Copper Man.

Copper Man

In some parts of the world, bodies placed in certain caves have air-dried rapidly and turned into mummies. In Palermo, Sicily, there is an underground burial cave called the Capuchin Catacombs. Its walls are lined with some 8,000 mummies of men, women, and children who died in the 1800s. All are dressed in their best clothes, their bodies preserved by the dryness of the air.

**VOCABULARY**
**trade**—job.
**coiled**—woven in a series of rings.
**hauling**—carrying.
**rawhide**—leather.
**stained**—colored.

**Mummies in a catacomb**

RESPONSE NOTES

Indian mummies have been found in the caves of Kentucky. One, for example, was discovered lying on a ledge in Salts Cave in 1875. Apparently the salts of the cave had absorbed moisture from the air and the movement of dry air had mummified the body. Named Little Alice, the mummy was exhibited for many years before being taken to the University of Kentucky in 1958. There careful examination showed that Little Alice was actually a boy who had died at the age of nine or ten. Carbon-14 dating gave an age for the mummy, now known as Little Al, of about 2,000 years.

**STOP AND RECORD**

Record information you want to remember about Little Al.

Little Al

**STOP AND RECORD**

The dry climate of the American Southwest, especially of Arizona, produced a number of well-preserved Indian mummies. Some of the earliest belonged to the Basket Makers, a group of wanderers who lived in caves and rock shelters of the region between A.D. 100 and 700.

**VOCABULARY**

**examination**—act of looking at closely.
**Carbon-14 dating**—determining how old something is by the amount of a type of carbon it contains.

**"Mummies"** continued

These mummies seem to have been made on purpose, to have been placed in caves so that the bodies would be preserved. With the mummies were various goods—sandals, beads, baskets, weapons, pipes. These may mean that the Basket Makers believed in a life after death and were providing the dead with what they might need. So far no one knows. Nor does anyone yet know why only some persons were chosen to become cave mummies—among them infants, children, women, and men—when most of the dead were buried in pits.

RESPONSE NOTES

STOP AND RECORD

Record information you want to remember about the Basket Makers.

Basket Makers

**VOCABULARY**
**providing**—giving.

Return to the **L** space of your K-W-L Chart and write what you learned from the selection.

**A. ORGANIZE DETAILS** Use the Venn diagram below to show how Egyptian mummies and mummies from other cultures are similar and different.

1. In the left circle, write information about Egyptian mummies. Look back at your notes in "Mummies."
2. In the right circle, write information about mummies from other cultures.
3. In the center, write what they have in common.

**A Native-American man pictured with a mummy**

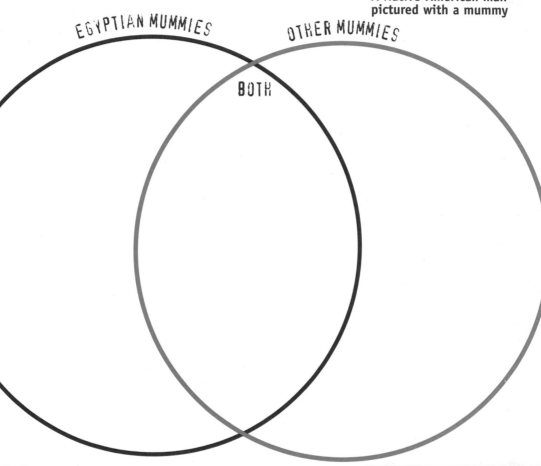

EGYPTIAN MUMMIES    OTHER MUMMIES

BOTH

**B. WRITE A TOPIC SENTENCE** Prepare to write a compare and contrast paragraph.

1. Review the Venn diagram above.
2. Write a topic sentence that tells how the mummies are either alike or different.

### TOPIC SENTENCE

## IV. WRITE

Write a **compare and contrast paragraph** about different kinds of mummies.

1. Start your paragraph with a topic sentence.
2. Organize your paragraph by giving details first about one kind of mummy and then about another.
3. Use the Writers' Checklist to help you revise.

## WRITERS' CHECKLIST

### SUBJECT/VERB AGREEMENT

☐ Did you check that subjects and verbs work together, or agree? Plural subjects require plural verbs, and singular subjects require singular verbs. EXAMPLES:
*Mummies is fascinating.* (incorrect)
*Mummies are fascinating.* (correct)

# V. WRAP-UP

What made "Mummies" easy or difficult for you to read?

**READERS' CHECKLIST**

**EASE**

☐ Was the passage easy to read?

☐ Were you able to read it smoothly and without difficulty?

# Jan Hudson

**J**an Hudson studied law in Canada before beginning her writing career. Her interest in Native American history inspired her to write her first novel, *Sweetgrass*. This highly praised novel tells the story of a young Native-American girl growing up.

Do you ever "see" what's happening as you read? Do you make a movie in your mind of the action, characters, and setting? Mental movies like that can help you keep track of what happens.

## I. BEFORE YOU READ

"Summer Berries" is a story about growing up. Think about this theme before you begin reading the story.
**1.** Look at the organizer below.
**2.** Record your thoughts and ideas in the boxes.

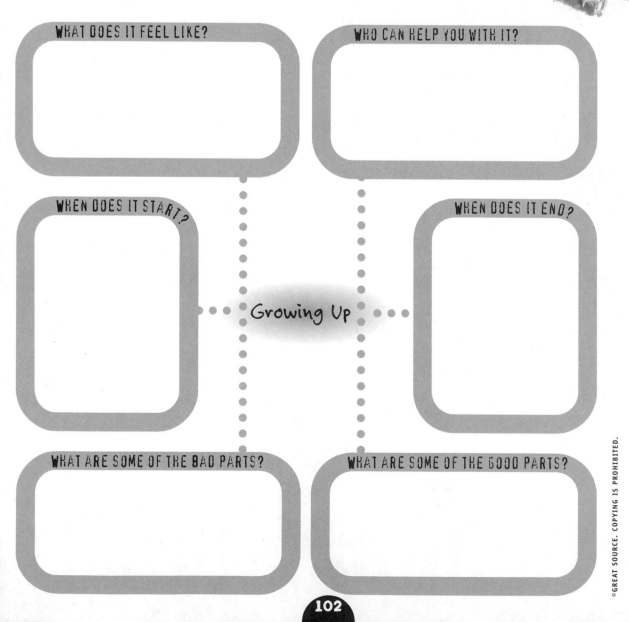

WHAT DOES IT FEEL LIKE?

WHO CAN HELP YOU WITH IT?

WHEN DOES IT START?

WHEN DOES IT END?

Growing Up

WHAT ARE SOME OF THE BAD PARTS?

WHAT ARE SOME OF THE GOOD PARTS?

# READ

Now read "Summer Berries" by Jan Hudson.

**1. Visualize** the people, places, and things Hudson describes.

**2.** Draw sketches of what you "see" in the Response Notes.

## "Summer Berries" from *Sweetgrass* by Jan Hudson

"What do you mean, Pretty-Girl?" I asked as we gathered strawberries that early summer morning. "Who could your parents want you to marry except Shy-Bear?"

"They will not say who they have chosen for me. Probably some old man. And everyone will <u>shame</u> me for not being happy to marry."

It was still exciting—my first friend-to-be-married! Pretty-Girl could not know how I would have <u>sacrificed</u> a finger to be in her place. I was fifteen, and she was thirteen—but she was the one whose parents had announced her marriage.

"But you and your Shy-Bear have cared for each other for two summers. Almost as long as I have cared for Eagle-Sun. And everyone has seen you together. Your parents must have noticed; everyone else has."

I sighed with happiness as we picked the small, <u>fragrant</u> berries. We had to be careful or else the strawberry blood would <u>stain</u> this perfect day. Sun, sand, <u>sage</u> and small red

EXAMPLE:

### VOCABULARY

**shame**—disgrace; make to feel wrong or foolish.
**sacrificed**—given up.
**fragrant**—nice smelling.
**stain**—ruin.
**sage**—a plant with grayish-green leaves often used in cooking.

**"Summer Berries"** continued

berries—a bird sang to us from a rosebrush clump, joyfully—the pattern of our lives.

All things moved as they should. Our lives seemed fixed as in a beaded design or the roundness of an old tale told on winter nights. Time would soon make women of us in marriage.

A few details of Pretty-Girl's story still sounded a little odd to me, though.

"Exactly what did your mother and father say to you?" I asked.

"Father said nothing. Mother told me. She just said that I should start sewing a new pair of <u>moccasins</u>, right for a bride."

# stop+think

List details you have learned so far.

Pretty-Girl

Sweetgrass

# stop+think

"And then?"

"And then she said she would make a good new dress. Then she went out of the <u>tipi</u>. Nothing more, Sweetgrass."

**VOCABULARY**
**moccasins**—soft leather slippers worn by Native Americans.
**tipi**—tepee; cone-shaped tent used by some Native Americans.

How <u>dully</u> she said it. Pretty-Girl kept picking the strawberries as steady as could be. Her little hands pulled at them as <u>daintily</u> as a deer <u>plucking</u> grass in a <u>meadow</u>. She had big eyes like a deer too, and beautiful long hair. I wished I looked like that.

"Don't you understand, Sweetgrass? My parents will not give me to Shy-Bear."

## stop-t-think

Add new details you have learned about Pretty-Girl and Sweetgrass.

Pretty-Girl          Sweetgrass

## stop-t-think

"Why not? You should ask them." I reached out and touched her shoulder. "Tell them—"

She shrugged my hand off. "You know how poor my family is. Shy-Bear does not have half the horses Father could get for me from some older man."

"Pretty-Girl—"

"Some older man with ten wives already, I bet that is what has been chosen for me!" The words tumbled out of her. "I will be the slavewife and clean buffalo <u>hides</u> all day and do all the hardest work. No one will ever be kind to me. Everything will always be awful until the babies come and even then it will still

**VOCABULARY**
**dully**—without interest.
**daintily**—gently.
**plucking**—pulling up.
**meadow**—grassy field.
**hides**—skins.

be bad. How I wish I did not have to. Oh, I would rather be dead than married!"

Tears fell on the berries. Tears are the wrong way to <u>greet</u> the marriage that every <u>Blackfoot</u> girl longs for. What could I say to make her act the right way?

"So your parents are giving you a new dress to go to your husband in. How lucky you are!"

Pretty-Girl said nothing.

"What kind of decorations are on the dress? Did your mother say?"

My friend looked up. She had decided not to cry, after all.

"What difference does the dress make? I want to know *who* I am going to wear it for!" She hid her face again.

# stop+think

Add any new details you have learned.

Pretty-Girl

Sweetgrass

# stop+think

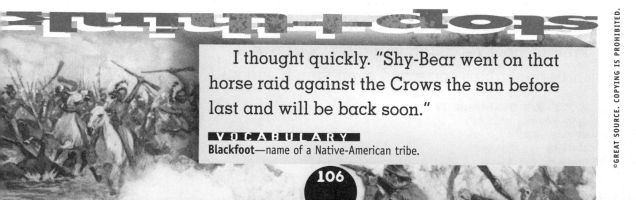

I thought quickly. "Shy-Bear went on that horse raid against the Crows the sun before last and will be back soon."

**VOCABULARY**
**Blackfoot**—name of a Native-American tribe.

**"Summer Berries"** continued

**R e s p o n s e    N o t e s**

"But he will not be able to bring back enough horses."

"Well, even so, you will not be treated like a slavewife. A new wife, perhaps. Especially one as beautiful as you."

"No?"

"How could anyone not love and honor you more than his other wives? You are as beautiful as a great chief's daughter in an old story. Remember all the things men have given to beautiful women. . . ."

"It will not happen. This is not a story."

"Of course it will. Please feel better now." I gave her a hug. All her <u>sorrow</u> made me feel strange inside.

"You do not understand, Sweetgrass. You are spoiled."

Spoiled! I always hear this. My almost-mother Bent-Over-Woman says Father gives me too much attention because I am his only daughter. Aside from my <u>obnoxious</u> almost-brother Otter, now twelve summers old, there have only been babies in our tipi. And when they die young, they are not counted. This is supposed to explain why my father lets me do what I want most of the time. A good Blackfoot girl is always <u>obedient</u>, quiet, hard-working, and she never says what she feels.

When I say what I feel, my father just laughs at me. My mother, people have said,

**V O C A B U L A R Y**
**sorrow**—sadness.
**obnoxious**—unpleasant; annoying.
**obedient**—doing what is asked.

©GREAT SOURCE. COPYING IS PROHIBITED.

*"Summer Berries"* continued

was Father's favorite of the three sisters he married. Who knows if that is so? I was only a baby when she died, too young to know anything. Only Almost-Mother is left now and she never talks about her sisters.

And Father gives me all the little things I want.

# stop+think

Add any new details you have learned.

Pretty-Girl

Sweetgrass

# stop+think

But he only gives me the little things—never the big ones. In important things like marriage, my parents treat me like a child. But I will be sixteen next summer. Then I will probably be the oldest unmarried girl among all the Bloods—even among all three Blackfoot tribes together—if Father does not stop finding <u>excuses</u> to keep me at home!

**VOCABULARY**
**excuses**—reasons.

# GATHER YOUR THOUGHTS

**A. DISCUSS** Get together in a reading group to discuss the story.

1. Ask yourselves some questions about "Summer Berries."
2. Write your own ideas about each question below before beginning the discussion.

**1. What is your reaction to "Summer Berries"?**

_____

_____

**2. What advice do you have for Pretty-Girl? for Sweetgrass?**

_____

_____

**3. Is there a time in your own life when you disagreed with the plans your family had for you? What happened?**

_____

_____

**B. ORGANIZE A PARAGRAPH** Plan to write a personal experience paragraph.

1. Use the chart below to organize a paragraph about a time when you disagreed with your family.
2. Write or jot your notes in the chart below.

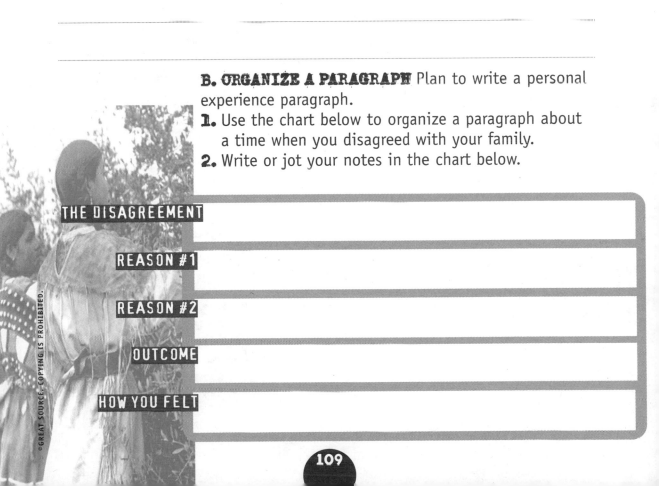

| THE DISAGREEMENT | |
| --- | --- |
| REASON #1 | |
| REASON #2 | |
| OUTCOME | |
| HOW YOU FELT | |

## IV. WRITE

Write a **personal experience paragraph** about a time you disagreed with your family's plans for you.

**1.** Explain the disagreement, your reasons for disagreeing, how it was resolved, and how you felt.

**2.** Use the Writers' Checklist to help you revise.

## V. WRAP-UP

Do you think "Summer Berries" is well written? Why or why not?

# 12: Summer Berries continued

If you see dark clouds and feel rain in the air, what do you do? You probably grab an umbrella before you go out. This is because you anticipate what will happen next. You expect rain to fall. When you read, you also anticipate and make guesses about what will happen next.

## BEFORE YOU READ

With a reading partner, review the first part of "Summer Berries" on pages 103-108.
1. Then complete the Anticipation Guide below.
2. Discuss your answers with your partner. If you disagree about a prediction, try to figure out why.

## Anticipation Guide

1. SWEETGRASS WILL CONVINCE PRETTY-GIRL TO MARRY THE MAN HER FATHER HAS CHOSEN FOR HER.

     1    2    3    4    5    6    7    8    9    10

definitely won't happen               definitely will happen

2. SWEETGRASS WILL TELL PRETTY-GIRL TO RUN AWAY.

     1    2    3    4    5    6    7    8    9    10

definitely won't happen               definitely will happen

3. SWEETGRASS WILL ALLOW HER FATHER TO CHOOSE A HUSBAND.

     1    2    3    4    5    6    7    8    9    10

definitely won't happen               definitely will happen

4. THE MEN WILL RETURN EMPTY-HANDED FROM THE RAID AGAINST THE CROWS.

     1    2    3    4    5    6    7    8    9    10

definitely won't happen               definitely will happen

5. PRETTY-GIRL WILL BE ALLOWED TO MARRY THE MAN SHE CHOOSES.

     1    2    3    4    5    6    7    8    9    10

definitely won't happen               definitely will happen

With your reading partner, take turns reading the next part of "Summer Berries" aloud.

**1.** Pay special attention to information that helps you understand the plot, characters, and theme.

**2.** In the Response Notes, write your **predictions** about what will happen next.

**Response Notes**

## "Summer Berries" (continued) from *Sweetgrass*
### by Jan Hudson

I stood up and pulled a flowering blade of <u>sweetgrass</u> from a little clump. That is my name, Sweetgrass. It is ordinary to look at, but it is as fragrant as the spring.

Sun shone on us. "Take this," I said to Pretty-Girl.

She twirled the grass in her hand, half-smiling, then tucked it into her thick hair and pulled some more for me. I <u>wove</u> them into my braids. My hair was burning hot and the sweetgrass sent out a <u>dizzying</u> perfume into the morning air.

"My father will <u>arrange</u> a marriage for me, too. Maybe this summer at the Sun Dance. Next summer for sure."

"Perhaps," said Pretty-Girl.

"Next summer, you will see. You and I will climb from the river together to pick strawberries, and we will be carrying our own

**EXAMPLE:**
Sweetgrass won't like the person her father picks.

**VOCABULARY**
**sweetgrass**—grass that smells good.
**wove**—tied.
**dizzying**—mind-spinning.
**arrange**—set up.

"**Summer Berries**" continued

babies on our backs. We will tell each other about our husbands and the fine horses that they own."

Promises hung <u>shimmering</u> in the future like glowing berries above sandy soil as we gathered our bags for the walk home. We had to hurry as the warriors would be back soon.

Many tipis, maybe even twenty, stood below us on the green campsite. My people were gathering together on their way to the Sun Dance. Oh, summer is the best time of the year!

I sang a little and Pretty-Girl smiled at me. I smiled back. She looked happy now.

What do Pretty-Girl and Sweetgrass want most out of life?

| PRETTY-GIRL | SWEETGRASS |
|---|---|
| | |

"I would bet if you look at your husband with your big eyes . . ." I began.

"You would bet on anything," laughed Pretty-Girl. "Worse than your almost-brother, Otter. You will lose everything you own someday."

"Never!"

"Yes, you will. Was it not an uncle of yours who lost his last horse playing knucklebone

**VOCABULARY**
shimmering—shining.

and then had to walk until someone lent him another?"

She <u>distracted</u> me by leaning over to poke at a big crumbling skull half-buried in the soft clay. You will often see that kind of bone in the Red Deer River badlands. Bigger than buffalo bones, and heavy. Almost like rocks.

And <u>eerie</u>.

"Pretty-Girl! Stay away from those old bones."

"Would not the people of the old-time <u>feast</u> well on buffalo this size?" she mused. "Maybe old-time people killed them for their Sun Dance."

"My grandmother says when her mother was young, there was no Sun Dance at all."

"Then where did all our heroes get their power, if not from their offerings to Sun? In the old times, I mean. Who but Sun would give them victory? There must have been a Sun Dance."

## stop+think

What words would you use to describe each of the girls?

| PRETTY-GIRL | SWEETGRASS |
| --- | --- |
|  |  |

| VOCABULARY |
| --- |
| **distracted**—took attention away from. |
| **eerie**—scary. |
| **feast**—eat. |

All I wanted to think about was the next Sun Dance. Soon my sweetheart, my hoped-to-be-sweetheart, would ride down from the north to brighten my days. Our camp would join his, almost any day now. Hurry faster, Eagle-Sun.

I slipped into a daydream and didn't even notice how far we had walked until Pretty-Girl grabbed my arm.

"Look, Sweetgrass! Look!"

She was pointing to the jagged horizon.

I squinted into the light and saw our returning warriors galloping their horses down the cliff path.

Their hair was flowing in the wind, colored streamers flying from horses and men alike. Brown arms were raised in victory. We could faintly hear the screams of the captured stallions and mares driven ahead of the raiders. The young men's bodies were graceful mysteries in their distance and in their power.

"A good raid!" I cried. Many horses rode with them, many horses to repay the older men who had helped start their careers. Many horses, at last, to pay a father to soften the loss of his young daughter in marriage.

### VOCABULARY

**jagged**—rough; uneven.
**horizon**—line at which the earth and sky appear to meet.
**stallions**—adult male horses.
**mares**—female horses.

"No one is hurt," Pretty-Girl breathed, "or they would not be racing, would they?"

"Of course not!"

Otter had gone on his first horse raid with Five-Killer's nephew, Open-Metal. What nerve in one so young! I hurried faster without admitting I cared how my almost-brother had done.

## stop+think

What does each girl want the result of the horse raid to be?

| PRETTY-GIRL | SWEETGRASS |
|---|---|
|  |  |

## stop+think

"Hurry," I cried. Pretty-Girl laughed a little as she jogged the few steps to catch up. I continued my reassurances. "I bet if you look at your man with those big eyes of yours and laugh like that, and let him smell the sweetgrass in your hair, I bet he will *have* to love you."

I heard a shout and turned to see Pretty-Girl sprawling on the ground. She had slipped in the soft clay.

"Father will marry me to Five-Killer," she wept. "I saw Five-Killer's nephew, the one who went on the raid."

"So?"

### VOCABULARY
**reassurances**—calming words.
**sprawling**—lying down with arms and legs spread out.

"So he was tying the best horses to Five-Killer's tipi. I just now saw it, in my mind. Father will want those beautiful horses more than anything. He'll marry me to Five-Killer and that is all."

It was a true <u>omen</u>. Pretty-Girl saw it and she felt it inside her. That was what was going to be.

After all, I breathed silently to myself, nothing very bad could happen. And the worst that could happen to Pretty-Girl could not happen to me. Despite her beauty, she was *kimataps*—from a poor family. But my father had been a celebrated warrior when he was young, until his leg was permanently <u>injured</u> from being thrown by his horse one day on a hunting <u>expedition</u>. Everyone knew the proud name of Shabby-Bull. He would never make his only daughter a slavewife, no matter how many horses he was offered.

I would make Father do what I wanted. I would find the signs, the power to control my own days. I would make my life be what I wanted.

## V O C A B U L A R Y
**omen**—sign of an event to come.
**injured**—hurt.
**expedition**—journey.

Return to the Anticipation Guide on page 111 and decide how accurate your predictions were.

# III. GATHER YOUR THOUGHTS

**A. EVALUATE** Think about the plot, characters, and theme of "Summer Berries."

**1.** Look back over the whole story.

**2.** Circle the number below that best describes your reactions.

### "SUMMER BERRIES"

● THE PLOT IS

| 1 | 2 | 3 | 4 | 5 |
|---|---|---|---|---|
| boring | | OK | | exciting |

● THE CHARACTERS ARE

| 1 | 2 | 3 | 4 | 5 |
|---|---|---|---|---|
| not interesting | | fairly interesting | | very interesting |

● THE THEME IS

| 1 | 2 | 3 | 4 | 5 |
|---|---|---|---|---|
| hard to understand | | kind of clear | | worth thinking about |

**B. DEVELOP AN OPINION** Get ready to write a review of either the plot, characters, or theme of "Summer Berries."

**1.** Use your evaluation above to help you state a clear opinion.

**2.** Then write 2–3 reasons to support your opinion.

My opinion:

My reasons:

1.

2.

3.

# IV. WRITE

Write a **review** of the plot, characters, or theme of "Summer Berries."

**1.** Begin with a statement of your overall opinion. Then give 2–3 details to support your point.

**2.** Use the Writers' Checklist to help you revise.

## WRITERS' CHECKLIST

### COMMAS

☐ Did you use commas to set off explanatory phrases? EXAMPLE: Sweetgrass's friend, called Pretty-Girl, put the flowers in her hair.

☐ Did you use commas to set off introductory phrases? EXAMPLE: Before last June, the girls had no worries.

☐ Did you use commas to set off interruptions? EXAMPLE: They were, of course, much younger then.

# V. WRAP-UP

What did Jan Hudson's story make you think about?

# Becoming Champions

Becoming Champions

No matter how talented you are, it takes a lot of hard work to become a champion. Some people work their entire lives to become a champion. But staying on top can be just as difficult as getting there.

Jackie Robinson

Sammy Sosa

Have you heard of Sammy Sosa? How much do you know about him? You may know how many home runs he's hit, but do you know what he's really like? One of the reasons we read is to find out information.

## I. BEFORE YOU READ

Skimming is one good way to get information from what you read.

1. Skim through the selection.
2. Underline the 2 most important words in each line of the first and last paragraphs.
3. Then answer the questions below.

**SKIMMING**

SELECTION TITLE: _____    AUTHOR: _____

_____

WHAT IS SAMMY SOSA LIKE?

_____

_____

WHAT IS THIS SELECTION ABOUT?

_____

_____

WHAT 3 THINGS DO I ALREADY KNOW ABOUT THIS TOPIC?

1. _____

2. _____

3. _____

HOW MUCH WILL I LIKE THIS SELECTION?

| a little | | | | | | | | a lot | |
|---|---|---|---|---|---|---|---|---|---|
| 1 | 2 | 3 | 4 | 5 | 6 | 7 | 8 | 9 | 10 |

# II. READ

Now read "A Better Life," part of a biography of Sammy Sosa.

1. **Highlight** or **mark** facts or details that you think are interesting.
2. In the Response Notes, note characteristics of Sosa and his life.

## "A Better Life" by Bill Gutman

Samuel Peralta Sosa was born in the Dominican town of San Pedro de Macoris on November 12, 1968. He was the fifth of seven children born to Juan Montero and Mireya Sosa, a hardworking couple who wanted only the best for their growing family. In young Sammy's earliest years he followed the other kids around, playing in the fields, often running barefoot through the streets, and sometimes seeing as many horse-drawn carts as automobiles. But he was still too young to know about baseball heroes, and the fact that sports and education could pave the way to a better life.

**RESPONSE NOTES**

EXAMPLE:
—a big family!

**STOP AND RETELL**

What was Sammy's childhood like?

........................................................

........................................................

........................................................

**VOCABULARY**

**San Pedro de Macoris**—a town in the southeastern part of the Dominican Republic, which is in the West Indies.

RESPONSE NOTES

But for Sammy and the rest of his family, things changed suddenly a short time later. When Sammy was just seven, his father died, and life quickly became a struggle just to <u>survive</u>. Mother and seven children lived in a home that was the <u>equivalent</u> of a one-bedroom apartment. Yet the cramped conditions only served to bring the family closer together and <u>instill</u> in them an iron will to overcome any and all <u>adversities</u>. Mireya Sosa began delivering food to workers at San Pedro's <u>textile</u> factories. She didn't make nearly enough money doing this, so all the children chipped in as well. Young Sammy began shining shoes for the equivalent of twenty cents. He also sold oranges and washed cars. All the money he made went immediately to his mother, as did the earnings of the other children.

**STOP AND RETELL**

Why did Sammy's mother go to work?

........................................................................

........................................................................

........................................................................

........................................................................

**VOCABULARY**
**survive**—stay alive.
**equivalent**—same as.
**instill**—put.
**adversities**—hard times.
**textile**—cloth.

**"A Better Life"** continued

Sammy sometimes made as much as two dollars a day to help his family pay the bills and buy groceries. Ironically, he once washed the car of George Bell, another native of San Pedro de Macoris, who would become an outstanding player for the Toronto Blue Jays in the early 1980s. But Sammy still wasn't thinking about baseball. While kids in the United States were already playing Little League, wearing colorful uniforms and learning the game on neatly manicured fields, Sammy and many others in the Dominican were working day after day just hoping to make a few dollars. Later, when people would ask Sammy about the pressure of playing in the majors, he always looked back at his roots.

"Pressure is when you have to shine shoes and sell oranges just to make sure there's enough to eat at the next meal," he would say. "That's the real pressure."

STOP AND THINK

How did Sammy spend his time when he was young?

.................................................................................

.................................................................................

.................................................................................

**VOCABULARY**
manicured—trimmed.
roots—background; the way he grew up.

RESPONSE NOTES

As Sammy approached his teen years he still hadn't played any baseball. In fact, the first sport that drew his interest was boxing—another sport that is popular in Latin American countries. When young Sammy put on the gloves and <u>sparred</u> with his friends, his mother became very upset. She didn't like to see her son being hit.

"He would tell me not to worry," Mireya Sosa said, "that it was nothing. And I would tell him, 'My son, for a mother it's a lot.'"

When he was about fourteen, one of his older brothers suggested he try playing baseball for the first time. He didn't have a glove, so he had to make do with an old milk carton turned inside out. It was apparent from the start that he had a feel for the game and some natural talent. And Sammy also remembered something else.

**STOP AND RETELL**

What happened when Sammy first started playing baseball?

........................................................................

........................................................................

........................................................................

........................................................................

**VOCABULARY**
**sparred**—boxed playfully.

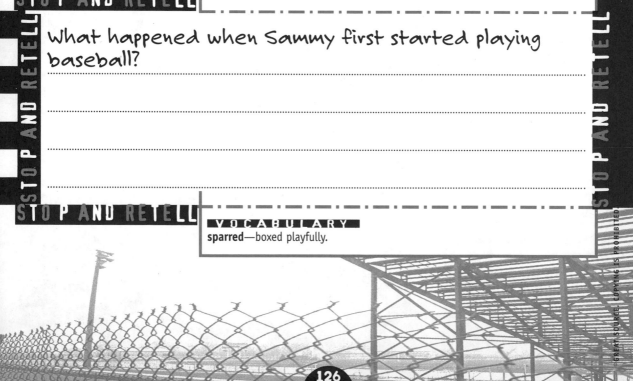

**"A Better Life"** continued

"I would see major league players from the Dominican, such as Joaquin Andujar, Julio Franco, and George Bell. They would build beautiful houses. People would come up to them. They were always in the middle of a crowd. And I can remember thinking it would be nice to live like that."

**STOP AND RETELL STOP AND RETELL STOP AND RETELL**

What did Sammy think when he started playing baseball?

## III. GATHER YOUR THOUGHTS

**A. CHOOSE A TOPIC** Get ready to write a speech about someone you admire. It could be a sports star, musician, author, or anyone else.

| A person I admire: | |
|---|---|

**B. ORGANIZE INFORMATION** Plan your speech on the index cards below.

---

**#1**

topic

**I. EARLY YEARS**

born when and where:



information about family:



---

**#2**

topic

**II. SCHOOL YEARS**

important events:

accomplishments:

challenges:

---

**#3**

topic

**III. ADULT YEARS**

important events:

accomplishments:

challenges:

---

## IV. WRITE

Write a **speech** about a person you admire.
1. Begin with a topic sentence.
2. Use your notes on page 128 to organize the speech into 3 paragraphs.
3. Use the Writers' Checklist to help you revise.

I admire                              because

> **Use this paragraph to introduce your topic and tell about the person's early years.**

> **Use the second paragraph to tell about the person's accomplishments and challenges as a child.**

Continue your writing on the next page.

## WRITERS' CHECKLIST

### CAPITALIZATION

☐ Did you capitalize all abbreviations?
EXAMPLES: *John D. Rockefeller, Samuel Watson, Jr.*

☐ Did you capitalize all titles? EXAMPLES:
*Mr. Bill Gutman, Dr. Kimberly Pezzola*

Continue your writing from the previous page.

Use the last paragraph to tell about the person's achievements and challenges as an adult.

_____

_____

_____

_____

_____

_____

_____

_____

## V. WRAP-UP

What is the author's message in "A Better Life"?

### READERS' CHECKLIST

**UNDERSTANDING**

☐ Did you understand the reading?

☐ Was the message or point clear?

☐ Can you restate what the reading is about?

_____

_____

_____

_____

_____

# 14: Jackie Robinson's First Game

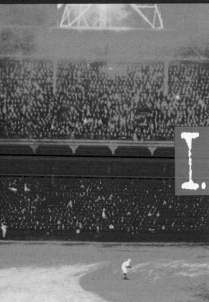

**What do shopping** for a present and reading a selection have in common? To do both of them, you first take the time to see what's there. Before you read, walk through the selection to help you know what to expect.

## BEFORE YOU READ

Thumb through "Jackie Robinson's First Game."
1. Circle the names of 2 or 3 people, places, and events on each page.
2. Put a star beside the most interesting picture you see.
3. Then answer the questions below.

What's special about Jackie Robinson?

When and where do the events take place?

What picture did you find interesting or unusual and why?

What questions do you have about the topic?

**WALK-THROUGH**

Now read "Jackie Robinson's First Game," part of the biography *Stealing Home*.

**1.** In the Response Notes, **react** and **connect** to what the author says.

**2.** Think especially about the kind of person Jackie Robinson was.

## RESPONSE NOTES

### "Jackie Robinson's First Game"
### by Barry Denenberg

The baseball season began in Florida, where white teams had their training camps. Like most Southern states in the 1940s, Florida was <u>segregated</u>. Whites were kept separate from blacks, especially when it came to traveling <u>accommodations</u>. Hotels, restaurants, and waiting rooms either didn't allow blacks or had an area <u>assigned</u> to them. Blacks could watch whites play baseball, but only from separate sections. And they could only watch whites play whites and blacks play blacks. Competition between the races on the playing fields was strictly forbidden— not only by <u>custom</u>, but by law. <u>Rickey</u> was aware of this, but he couldn't do anything about where spring training began. He did as much groundwork as possible over the winter, talking with local officials to make Jackie's arrival as smooth as possible.

EXAMPLE:
Robinson must have been very nervous. I would have been.

**VOCABULARY**

**segregated**—separated into groups of blacks and whites, with no mixing between the two.
**accommodations**—places to stay overnight and places to eat.
**assigned**—set apart.
**custom**—tradition.
**Rickey**—Branch Rickey, the commissioner of baseball.

**"Jackie Robinson's First Game"** continued

The Florida newspapers made it clear that Jackie was not welcomed. They liked their segregated Southern ways, and now here *he* was to change all that. Hotel and restaurant owners said they weren't going to treat Jackie Robinson differently from any other black.

The <u>Royals</u>' first game in Jacksonville was cancelled. The head of the playground and recreation committee said that whites and blacks could not compete against each other on city-owned playgrounds. In another game the chief of police walked right on the field and informed the Montreal manager that Robinson had to be removed. To keep the peace he was.

**STOP AND RECORD**

Record the order of events on this organizer.

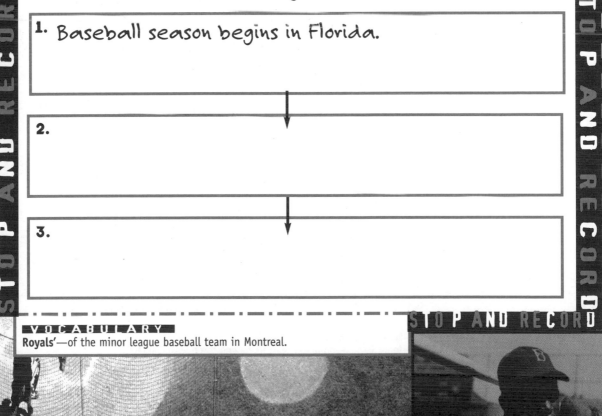

1. Baseball season begins in Florida.

2.

3.

**STOP AND RECORD**

**VOCABULARY**
**Royals'**—of the minor league baseball team in Montreal.

Rickey didn't want to become involved with legal issues in Florida—not if he could avoid it. "I'm going there to play ball, not to live," he said. He did whatever he could to avoid problems. He had Jackie and Rachel stay at the home of a black political leader. But Rickey knew they would have to make a stand somewhere. The president of the Montreal Royals issued a statement: "It will be all or nothing with the Montreal club. Jackie Robinson go[es] with the team, or there's no game." Rickey knew that Florida politicians were beginning to feel the heat put on them by Northern newspapers who were critical of what was going on. He also knew that he had economics on his side. Daytona city officials had acted better than most in making Jackie and the Royals feel welcome. Having the Dodgers spend spring training there every year brought a lot of money into the community. The officials were worried that the Dodgers might go somewhere else.

Jackie had so many things to worry about, he wasn't sure where to begin. While the tension swirled all around him, he struggled to concentrate on baseball. He still had to make the team. His first day at spring training reminded him of how he had felt his first day of school—nervous and unsure of himself.

**VOCABULARY**
**legal issues**—points or matters having to do with the law.
**economics**—the power of money.
**Dodgers**—baseball team in Brooklyn, New York.
**tension**—stress.
**concentrate**—think about; focus on.

**"Jackie Robinson's First Game"** continued

There were over 200 white ballplayers on the field, all trying out for a position. As far as baseball playing was concerned, Jackie was just one of the guys. When reporters asked him if he was after the Dodger shortstop position, Pee Wee Reese's job, he told them he was worried about making the *Montreal* club, not Brooklyn. He wanted to do well so badly that he tried too hard and developed a sore arm. He had to be switched to second, but his arm was too sore to make the throw from there, too. They moved him to first base. Now, on top of everything else, he was making his <u>debut</u> in spring training at a position he had never played before.

**STOP AND RECORD**

Record the next 3 events the author describes.

4.

5.

6.

**VOCABULARY**
**debut**—first appearance.

The exhibition season ended without any proof of Jackie's ability. He was plagued by a sore arm and his hitting was erratic. There was still plenty of doubts about his ability to play in the big leagues.

*April 18, 1946, Jersey City, New Jersey.* Jackie Robinson was about to play his first game in organized baseball. Thirty-five thousand fans jammed Roosevelt Stadium to watch the Royals play the Jersey City Giants. Newspaper reporters were out in full force. Jackie grounded out his first trip to the plate. But in the top of the third, with men on first and second, he hit the first pitch for a 340-foot three-run home run. In the fifth inning he bunted, stole second, and went to third on an infield out. With Rickey's instructions to be daring on the base paths buzzing in his ears, Jackie pranced off third base. When the pitcher began his windup he streaked for home, pulled up and ran back, sliding into third just in time. On his third pitch, the pitcher balked and Jackie scored. He singled his last time up and went to third when the

**VOCABULARY**

**exhibition season**—games played early in a baseball season for practice.
**plagued**—bothered.
**erratic**—not regular; all over the place.
**pranced**—walked or ran in a proud way.
**streaked**—ran quickly.
**balked**—stopped his pitching motion too suddenly.

**"Jackie Robinson's First Game"** continued

ball glanced off the second baseman's glove. Again he was balked home, bringing the crowd to its feet. Jackie Robinson's <u>reputation</u> as the most daring base runner in baseball history was beginning.

STOP AND RECORD

Record 4 more things that happen here.

> **7.**

> **8.**

> **9.**

> **10.**

**VOCABULARY**
**reputation**—opinion others have of a person.

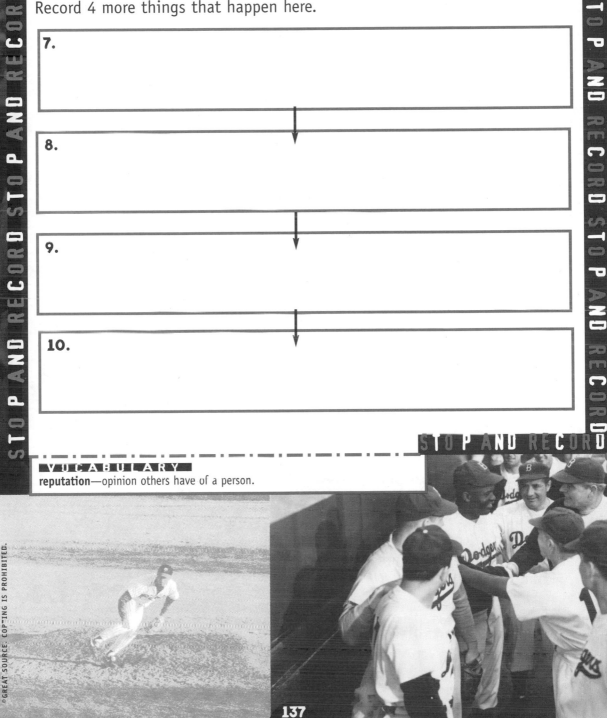

## GATHER YOUR THOUGHTS

**A. DESCRIBE** What kind of person was Jackie Robinson?

**1.** Write 4 of his qualities on the Character Map below.

**2.** Provide an example for each quality.

**CHARACTER MAP**

QUALITY:

EXAMPLE:

QUALITY:

EXAMPLE:

Jackie Robinson

QUALITY:

EXAMPLE:

QUALITY:

EXAMPLE:

**B. FORM A TOPIC SENTENCE** Prepare to write a biographical paragraph about Jackie Robinson. First, complete the topic sentence below by identifying 2 of Robinson's qualities.

The two finest qualities of Jackie Robinson are

and

## IV. WRITE

Write a **biographical paragraph** about Jackie Robinson.

1. Begin with your topic sentence. Tell what made him so great.
2. State one quality and give 2 details in support of it. Then state another quality and give 2 more details to support it.
3. End with a closing sentence that restates your overall feelings.
4. Use the Writers' Checklist to help you revise.

Continue your writing on the next page.

## WRITERS' CHECKLIST

### CAPITALIZATION

☐ Did you capitalize the names of specific buildings, monuments, institutions, companies, sports teams, and groups?
EXAMPLES: *Roosevelt Stadium, University of Florida, Brooklyn Dodgers*

☐ Did you capitalize the names of ethnic groups and languages? EXAMPLES: *Latino, American, Cuban*

Continue your writing from the previous page.

## V. WRAP-UP

What did this article about Jackie Robinson mean to you?

**READERS' CHECKLIST**

**MEANING**

- ❑ **Did you learn something from the reading?**
- ❑ **Did it affect you or make an impression?**

# Ancient Mexico

Emperor Moctezuma

Hernán Cortés

Ancient Mexico was thriving when the Spanish arrived in the early 1500s. The Aztecs welcomed the explorers from Europe at first, but soon began a bitter war. They fought to protect their way of life from European control. The ruins of ancient Mexico are now all that remain of the once flourishing Aztec people.

Have you heard the saying "A picture is worth a thousand words"? It means that pictures can give you a lot of information. By doing a picture walk before you read, you create a frame, or context, for what you are about to read.

## BEFORE YOU READ

Page through "The Strangers Arrive."

1. Look closely at each piece of art and read all of the captions.
2. Write the topic of the selection in the top box.
3. Then write at least 4 questions that come to mind after looking at the art.

**Cortés's men approaching Tenochtitlán**

**"The Strangers Arrive"**

TOPIC

QUESTION #1

QUESTION #2

QUESTION #3

QUESTION #4

# READ

Now read "The Strangers Arrive," from *Lost Temple of the Aztecs*.

**1.** As you read, pay attention to details that seem important.

**2. Clarify** key information that will help you answer your questions in the Response Notes.

**Response Notes**

## "The Strangers Arrive" by Shelley Tanaka

APRIL 1519

The ships came from the east. They just appeared on the <u>horizon</u> one day, as if they had dropped from the sky. They were bigger than any boats the people had ever seen, and they floated toward the shore like small mountains.

When <u>Moctezuma's</u> messengers saw the ships, they hurried back to <u>Tenochtitlán.</u>

"Strange people have come to the shores of the great sea," they told their ruler. "They have very light skin and long beards, and their hair only comes down to their ears. They sit on huge deer that carry them wherever they want to go."

EXAMPLE:
Moctezuma=
Aztec ruler

## stop+predict

What will the people on the ships want?

**VOCABULARY**
**horizon**—line where the earth and sky appear to meet.
**Moctezuma's**—of the ruler of the Aztec Indians in Mexico in the 1500s.
**Tenochtitlán**—ancient Aztec city.

Moctezuma listened to the news in silence. His mind raced.

Quetzalcoatl has appeared! he thought. He has come back to reclaim his throne!

It was happening, just as the ancient prophecy had foretold. Long ago, according to legend, Quetzalcoatl, the great god of learning and creation, had sailed east on a raft of serpents to a mysterious land across the ocean. But he had promised to come back, and this was the predicted year of his return.

Moctezuma knew there had already been signs that things were not well with the gods, that some momentous change was about to come to his people. Two years before, a great tongue of fire had streaked across the night sky, like a spear plunged into the very heart of the heavens. At dawn, the sun destroyed the fire, but the next night it appeared again. And so it went on for the better part of a year, and each night the people watched with terror. Would the sun, the source of all life, continue to destroy the fire? Might the sun one day stop rising?

**VOCABULARY**
**Quetzalcoatl**—an Aztec god.
**reclaim**—take back.
**ancient prophecy**—old story that predicts things in the future.
**serpents**—snakes.
**momentous**—very important.
**plunged**—thrown into.
**terror**—fear.

**"The Strangers Arrive"** continued

There were other signs of death and ruin. Temples burst into flames. The great lake that surrounded Tenochtitlán swirled and bubbled up as if it were boiling with rage. The nights echoed with the sound of a woman wailing.

Moctezuma was filled with fear and confusion at these unnatural happenings. The gods must be looking unfavorably on the richest and most powerful empire in the land.

And now, it seemed, one of the gods had returned. Quetzalcoatl had arrived.

JULY 1519

Moctezuma gathered his chiefs around him. "Our lord, Quetzalcoatl, has arrived at last. Hurry to meet him. Tell him that his servant Moctezuma has sent you to welcome him back to his throne, and take him these gifts."

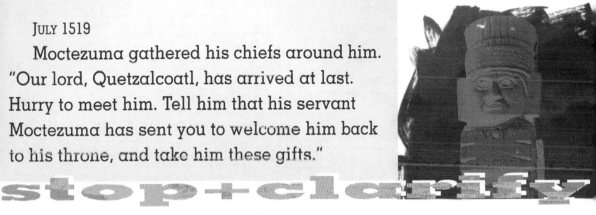

**An ancient Mexican totem**

## stop+clarify

Who does Moctezuma think has arrived?

stop+clarify

**"The Strangers Arrive"** continued

Moctezuma's messengers traveled to the coast. They placed their gifts in canoes and paddled out to where the huge ships floated offshore. The pale-skinned strangers let down a ladder, and the messengers climbed on board. They were taken to the leader, whom the strangers called <u>Cortés</u>. Surely he was Quetzalcoatl himself!

The messengers kissed the deck at Cortés's feet. "We bring these gifts from your servant Moctezuma," they told him. "He guards over your kingdom and keeps it safe for your return."

## stop+question

What questions do you have about Cortés?

_____

_____

_____

_____

_____

**VOCABULARY**
**Cortés**—a Spanish explorer who conquered the Aztecs in the 1500s.

**Cortés meeting the messengers of Moctezuma**

**"The Strangers Arrive"** continued

Then they adorned Cortés with a serpent mask made of <u>turquoise</u> and a <u>headdress</u> of <u>shimmering</u> blue-green <u>quetzal</u> feathers. They draped gold and <u>jade</u> bands around his neck, arms, and legs. They placed a cape of <u>ocelot</u> skin and sandals of glistening black <u>obsidian</u> at his feet, along with all the other gifts— serpent-head staffs and spears inlaid with green jade, masks, shields, and fans heavy with gold and turquoise.

Cortés looked at everything they had given him. "Are these your gifts of welcome?" he asked. "Is this all you have brought?"

"Yes, lord," the messengers replied. "This is everything."

## stop+question

What questions do you have about Cortés's first meeting with the Aztecs?

_____

_____

_____

_____

stop+question

### VOCABULARY

**turquoise**—light blue stone.
**headdress**—fancy covering or decoration worn on the head.
**shimmering**—shining.
**quetzal**—bird with bronze-green and red feathers.
**jade**—pale green or white stone.
**ocelot**—wildcat.
**obsidian**—black stone formed from volcanic lava.

**Hernán Cortés**

Cortés ordered his men to fasten irons around the messengers' ankles and necks. Then he fired a huge gun. The messengers had never seen such a sight. They fainted from fear and fell to the deck.

The strangers <u>revived</u> them with wine and food.

"I have heard about your people," Cortés said. "They say that one Aztec warrior can overpower twenty men. I want to see how strong you are." He gave them leather shields and iron swords. "Tomorrow at dawn, you will fight, and then we will find out the truth."

"But this is not the wish of our lord and your servant, Moctezuma," the messengers answered. "He has only told us to greet you and bring you gifts."

"You will do as I say," said Cortés. "Tomorrow morning we shall eat. After that you will prepare for <u>combat</u>."

**VOCABULARY**
**revived**—made healthy again.
**combat**—fighting.

# stop+summarize

How would you summarize what's happened?

_____

_____

_____

_____

_____

# III. GATHER YOUR THOUGHTS

**A. EXPLORE A TOPIC** Prepare to write an expository paragraph telling about either Moctezuma or Cortés.

**1.** First decide on your topic. (circle one)

MOCTEZUMA                    CORTÉS

**2.** Then decide where will you find information about your topic? Circle the 2 resources you like best.

LIBRARY BOOK                 INTERNET

ENCYCLOPEDIA                 MAGAZINE ARTICLE

**B. ORGANIZE RESEARCH** Now locate at least 2 specific sources about your topic. Organize information you find by taking notes that answer each of the questions below.

| My topic | |
|---|---|
| 1. WHO WAS HE? | |
| 2. WHERE AND WHEN DID HE LIVE? | |
| 3. WHAT DID HE DO? | |
| 4. HOW DID OTHERS FEEL ABOUT HIM? | |
| 5. WHY IS HE IMPORTANT TO REMEMBER? | |

# IV. WRITE

Write a short **expository paragraph** about Cortés or Moctezuma.

**1.** Refer to the notes from your organizer.

**2.** Remember to start with a topic sentence.

**3.** Use the Writers' Checklist to help you revise.

## WRITERS' CHECKLIST

### CONFUSING WORDS

☐ Did you use *it's* only as a contraction for "it is" and *its* as the possessive form of "it"? EXAMPLES: *It's clear that Cortés wanted to fight. He shot off a gun, and its sound scared everyone.*

☐ Did you use *their* as a possessive pronoun, *there* as an adverb to point out location, and *they're* as the contraction for "they are"? EXAMPLES: *There are the guards. They're famous for their discipline.*

# V. WRAP-UP

What parts of "The Strangers Arrive" were easy or difficult to read? Why?

## READERS' CHECKLIST

### EASE

☐ Was the passage easy to read?
☐ Were you able to read it smoothly and without difficulty?

_____

_____

_____

_____

_____

_____

_____

_____

_____

Would you like to travel around the world? You can do it through your reading. Reading can open up whole new worlds for you and teach you about people and places you've never dreamed of.

## I. BEFORE YOU READ

Think about the people and places you learned about in "The Strangers Arrive."

**1.** Then read each of the sentences below.

**2.** With a partner, put a 1 before the sentence that you think comes first in the following selection, a 2 before the sentence that comes next, and so on.

**3.** Then make a prediction about "The Great Moctezuma."

### Think-Pair-Share

_____ "Moctezuma was almost crazy with worry and indecision."

_____ "Moctezuma knew that this year was one of the times in the cycle of years that legend said Quetzalcoatl, the Plumed Serpent, might return to earth to rule his people."

_____ "After one week in Tenochtitlán, Hernán Cortés took Moctezuma and his family prisoners and made Moctezuma announce to all of the people that Cortés was now in charge."

_____ "When the Spanish finally arrived at the crest of the hill above Tenochtitlán in November, they could hardly believe their eyes."

_____ "The city and all of its treasures now belonged to the Spanish."

What will this selection be about?

_____

_____

_____

# II. READ

Read "The Great Moctezuma."

**1.** As you read, think of questions you have about Moctezuma, Cortés, or what's happening.

**2.** Write your **questions** in the Response Notes.

## "The Great Moctezuma"
### by Donna Walsh Shepherd

Moctezuma knew that this year was one of the times in the cycle of years that <u>legend</u> said Quetzalcoatl, the Plumed Serpent, might return to earth to rule his people. There had been many strange <u>omens</u> of his return during the past year. In the old <u>codices</u>, Quetzalcoatl had white skin and a beard and had sailed on a raft to the east. Could this be Quetzalcoatl coming back?

<u>Seers and soothsayers</u> began coming to Moctezuma. They had been having dreams, dreams of Tenochtitlán burning and falling apart stone by stone. Messengers brought more news of the strangers who were marching over the mountains to Tenochtitlán. The leader was called Hernán Cortés. Along the way he was knocking down <u>temples</u> of the brother and sister gods who had forced Quetzalcoatl to leave Mexico and replacing the temples with a

**EXAMPLE:**
Did anyone keep a list of the omens?

**VOCABULARY**

**legend**—a story that is passed down through the years.
**omens**—signs of events to come.
**codices**—manuscripts containing a body of laws.
**Seers** and **soothsayers**—people who see the future.
**temples**—places of worship.

cross. Surely, Moctezuma thought, these strangers were Quetzalcoatl or his representatives.

## stop+think

Why does Moctezuma believe that Cortés is Quetzalcoatl?

........................................................................

........................................................................

........................................................................

## stop+think

Moctezuma was almost crazy with worry and <u>indecision</u>. Some of his advisors said, "Attack. Do not let them in the city. We will be ruined." The two hundred thousand Aztec warriors could easily defeat the five hundred strangers. Others said, "Do not anger them. They must be gods and will destroy us if we displease them."

When the Spanish finally arrived at the crest of the hill above Tenochtitlán in November, they could hardly believe their eyes. In the valley below lay a huge city in the center of a lake. It was a city of beautiful <u>monuments</u>, gardens, and canals. It lay like a giant glistening jewel floating on the water. Never before had they seen such a beautiful and orderly city—not Paris, not London, not Madrid, not Rome. They were all villages

**VOCABULARY**
**indecision**—not being able to make up one's mind.
**monuments**—works or buildings, often of stone, built to honor someone.

compared to Tenochtitlán. More than a million people lived in the island city and on the shores of Lake Texcoco.

Moctezuma decided to greet Hernán Cortés and the Spaniards as friends and welcome them to Tenochtitlán with a celebration. The Spanish stayed in the palace reserved for important guests. They were given great feasts and beautiful gifts of gold, precious stones, embroidery, and featherworks. They were shown all of the city and allowed to visit the temples.

Soon Moctezuma realized that Cortés was not a representative of Quetzalcoatl, but he did not know what these strange people wanted.

## stop+think

What do you think Cortés wants?

......................................................................................

......................................................................................

......................................................................................

......................................................................................

## stop+think

Moctezuma hoped that if he gave the Spaniards enough presents they could be bribed to go away. He gave them more of the gold they seemed to like so much, including a helmet filled with gold dust and a gold carving

### VOCABULARY
**embroidery**—cloth stitched with decorative designs.
**bribed**—paid.

of the sun several feet in <u>diameter</u>. But the golden gifts only made the Spaniards want more. Moctezuma didn't know that the Spaniards felt they were on God's <u>mission</u> to save Indian souls and believed that any gold or wealth they might find was God's way of repaying them for their good deeds.

After one week in Tenochtitlán, Hernán Cortés took Moctezuma and his family prisoners and made Moctezuma announce to all of the people that Cortés was now in charge.

The city and all of its treasures now belonged to the Spanish. Cortés melted down beautifully carved gold jewelry and religious symbols and sent the gold and other Aztec treasures back to Spain.

## stop+think

What did Cortés do with the Aztec treasures? Why?

........................................................................................

........................................................................................

........................................................................................

........................................................................................

........................................................................................

**VOCABULARY**
**diameter**—width or measurement across a circle.
**mission**—goal.

**"The Great Moctezuma"** continued

Months later, during an Aztec holy day celebration when Cortés was temporarily gone from Tenochtitlán, Spanish soldiers began to fear that the dancing Aztecs were getting ready to attack. They <u>massacred</u> hundreds of unarmed dancers. <u>Chaos</u> followed. Somehow Moctezuma was killed—stoned by his own people, the Spanish said; murdered by the Spanish, said the Aztecs. Both Aztecs and Spanish, who had come to respect Moctezuma, <u>mourned</u> his death.

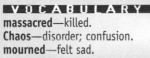

How did Cortés treat Moctezuma and his people?

..................................................................................................

..................................................................................................

..................................................................................................

..................................................................................................

**VOCABULARY**
**massacred**—killed.
**Chaos**—disorder; confusion.
**mourned**—felt sad.

**ORDER EVENTS** Like fiction, history often tells a story. When you read history, it's important to understand the sequence of events.

**1.** Use this organizer to summarize in order what happened to Moctezuma and Tenochtitlán.

**2.** Write a different event in every box.

Moctezuma hears that strangers are making their way toward Tenochtitlán.

## IV. WRITE

Write a **summary** of the events in "The Great Moctezuma."

**1.** Begin with a topic sentence and use details from your organizer.

**2.** Use the Writers' Checklist as you revise.

Continue your writing on the next page.

**WRITERS' CHECKLIST**

### COMMAS

☐ Did you use commas to set off explanatory phrases? EXAMPLE: *Quetzalcoatl, the Plumed Serpent, was described in legends.*

☐ Did you use commas between coordinate adjectives that aren't joined by and? EXAMPLES: *The brave, strong warriors were scared. The brave and strong warriors were scared.*

Continue your writing from the previous page.

V. WRAP-UP
**WRAP-UP**

What did "The Great Moctezuma" make you think about?

# Joseph Krumgold

**B**efore he was a writer of children's literature, Joseph Krumgold was a writer of movies. He has written screenplays for the major studios in Hollywood and has also directed documentary films. Krumgold based . . . *and now Miguel* on one of his own documentaries.

...and now Miguel

By JOSEPH KRUMGOLD
ILLUSTRATED BY JEAN CHARLOT

What do you want most right now? Have you ever wanted something but not been able to put your finger on it? That's just the way Miguel feels in "I Am Miguel."

 **BEFORE YOU READ**

Do a 1-minute quickwrite.

1. Write about what you want and need. Is there any difference between the two?

2. When you've finished, look over what you wrote.

3. Circle your most important ideas and share them with a partner.

**1-MINUTE QUICKWRITE**

**READ**

Now read "I Am Miguel," part of a novel by Joseph Krumgold.

**1.** As you read, **visualize** the scene the author describes.

**2.** Make sketches of what you "see" in the Response Notes.

### "I Am Miguel" from . . . and now Miguel
### by Joseph Krumgold

I am Miguel. For most people it does not make so much difference that I am Miguel. But for me, often, it is a very great trouble.

It would be different if I were Pedro. He is my younger brother, only seven years old. For Pedro everything is simple. Almost all the things that Pedro wants, he has—without much worry.

I wanted to find out how it was with him one day when we were in our private place near the Rio Pueblo, the river that goes through our farm. I asked him "Pedro, suppose you could have anything you want. Is there anything you want?"

"Ai, of course." He looked up from reaching below a rock in the river. In this way we catch trout, slowly feeling around in the quiet places beneath big stones. If the fish comes by, sliding soft against your hand, you can catch him. Pedro was just learning to fish like this.

EXAMPLE:

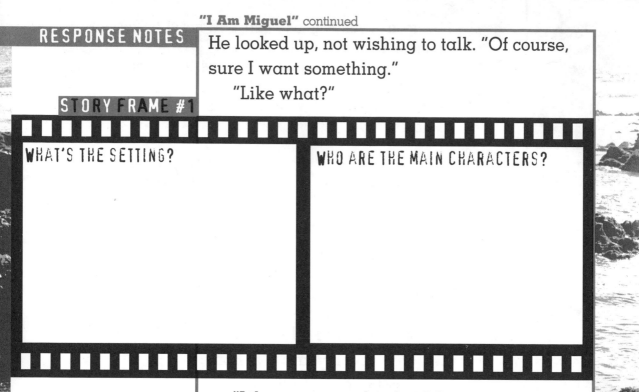

He looked up, not wishing to talk. "Of course, sure I want something."

"Like what?"

**STORY FRAME #1**

**WHAT'S THE SETTING?**

**WHO ARE THE MAIN CHARACTERS?**

"Like not so much school."

"School—yes. But that is something that you do not want."

"Like I say—not so much."

"Then what is it that you *do* want?"

"Shh!" He closed his eyes, moving his hand slowly, slowly in the water, holding his breath, with his tongue between his teeth.

Of a sudden he grabbed, splashing. He made a big <u>commotion</u> in the water. It was no good. Even before he took his hand out of the water, I knew it was empty.

"A good big trout, that's what I do want." Pedro looked at me like he was mad at me, like I spoiled his chance for the fish. "A good one, six inches big!"

**VOCABULARY**

**commotion**—noisy activity or confusion.

**"I Am Miguel"** continued

He was mad. He took a stone and threw it into the water with all his might.

So I caught him a trout. It is not so hard. You lay down with your hand in the water, in a place where there are shadows below the bank. You leave your hand there for a long time, until the fish see that it is nothing strange. Until they come by, even touching you. Until you can touch them, even rub them very lightly. They seem to like this, the fish, for you to rub them this way. Then when you feel them coming through your fingers, slowly you hold on to them, slowly but tight. Without any sudden move. And that's that.

I gave the fish to Pedro. It was almost six inches. He was happy with me again.

That's the way it is with Pedro. One such fish, not too big after all, and he is happy.

STORY FRAME #2

WHAT DID YOU LEARN ABOUT PEDRO AND MIGUEL FROM THE STORY ABOUT THE TROUT?

It is enough for him for everything to be like it is.

When the sun shines hot and dry and he can go swimming in the pool where the river goes around the farm of my Uncle Eli, that for Pedro is enough.

And when it rains, that too is enough. He is a great artist, Pedro. He sits in the kitchen when there is thunder outside, and all the pictures in his book he turns yellow and red and blue with his crayons.

If there is a ball, he will play ball. And if there is not, he will roll an old tire. No matter which, he is content.

It would be good to be Pedro. But how long can you stay seven years old? The trouble with me is that I am Miguel.

**STORY FRAME #3**

WHAT PROBLEM OR CONFLICT DO YOU THINK MIGUEL FACES?

# GATHER YOUR THOUGHTS

**A. PLAN** Joseph Krumgold wrote about a person who wishes he could be like his seven-year-old brother. Get ready to write a paragraph about a time you wanted something but couldn't have it.

**1.** Use the storyboards below to tell your story.

**2.** Draw a picture in each box. Underneath, write a sentence describing what you've drawn.

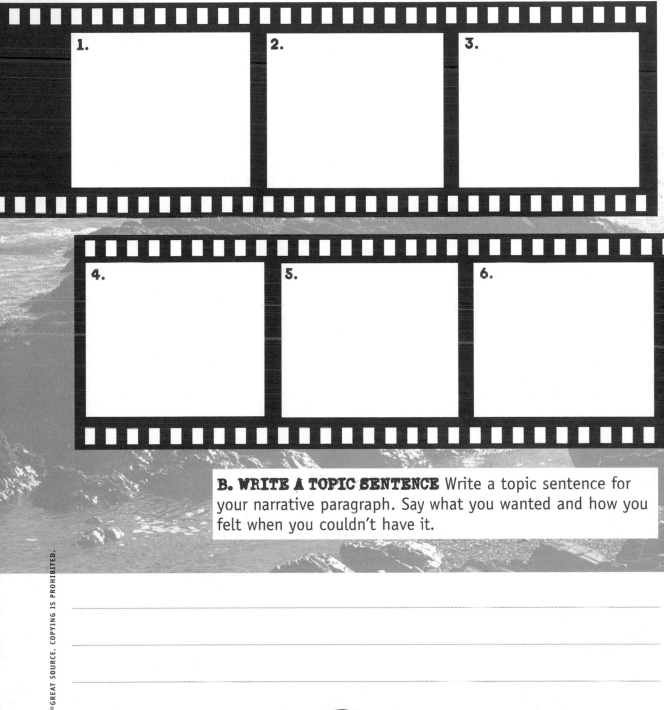

1.

2.

3.

4.

5.

6.

**B. WRITE A TOPIC SENTENCE** Write a topic sentence for your narrative paragraph. Say what you wanted and how you felt when you couldn't have it.

Write a **narrative paragraph** describing a time you wanted something but couldn't have it.

**1.** Open with your topic sentence and include details from your storyboard.

**2.** Review the Writers' Checklist before you revise.

## V. WRAP-UP

What did you like most about Joseph Krumgold's writing? What did you like least?

How often have you found yourself asking, "I wonder what will happen next?" When you answer this question, you make a prediction. Making predictions about movies, TV shows, and stories can help you get involved with what you're seeing and reading.

## BEFORE YOU READ

Get together with a partner before beginning to read the next part of the story of Miguel.

**1.** One of you should read aloud the first five paragraphs on the next page.

**2.** Then respond to the statements on the Anticipation Guide.

**3.** Share your answers with your reading partner. Then make a prediction about what will happen.

## ANTICIPATION GUIDE

### 1. Taking care of sheep is hard work.

A. Strongly Disagree    B. Disagree    C. Agree    D. Strongly Agree

### 2. Children want to impress their parents.

A. Strongly Disagree    B. Disagree    C. Agree    D. Strongly Agree

### 3. My parents don't understand I'm old enough to make my own decisions.

A. Strongly Disagree    B. Disagree    C. Agree    D. Strongly Agree

### 4. If I know your name, I know a lot about you.

A. Strongly Disagree    B. Disagree    C. Agree    D. Strongly Agree

### 5. Kids know best about what they need.

A. Strongly Disagree    B. Disagree    C. Agree    D. Strongly Agree

"Sangre de Cristo Mountains" will be about . . .

## READ

Take turns reading "Sangre de Cristo Mountains" with your partner.

1. Continue to make **predictions** about what will happen to Miguel.
2. Write your predictions in the Response Notes.

**"Sangre de Cristo Mountains"** from . . . *and now Miguel* by Joseph Krumgold

There is one thing to say right away about the Sangre de Cristo Mountains and it is this. They are wonderful.

I don't know if it is true but I have been told that if you are good all the time and if sometimes you pray, then you will go to heaven. Maybe this is so and maybe not.

But about the Sangre de Cristo Mountains I know for sure. If you are ready and the time comes, then that's all. You will go.

To get to be ready, it is first necessary to be of my family, a Chavez, and that I have come to be without even trying. Then, one must be a shepherd and know all about how to take care of the sheep. It is likewise a help to know how to bake bread and be a good cook as well as to ride a horse and shoot a gun and catch fish. When you can do these things then you are ready.

And all that must be done then is to wait until the time comes.

And it always does. Every year. It comes as sure as the time for the lambs to be born, and

EXAMPLE:
Miguel will learn to be a shepherd.

**VOCABULARY**
**Sangre de Cristo Mountains**—mountains in southern Colorado and New Mexico.
**shepherd**—person who keeps a flock of sheep.

the time for the <u>Fiesta de San Ysidro</u>, and then the <u>shearers</u> arrive and the wool is clipped. Just so sure as all these things happen, comes the time for the flock to go up into the Mountains of the Sangre de Cristo.

Then you will go along. If, that is, everyone knows you are ready.

But if they don't, then you must wait again for another whole year. And even another year and another.

Each year, after the last heavy snows are over, the time comes to show that I am ready and that it is different this year for me, Miguel, than it was last year. It is in this early part of the year that the new lambs are born.

**STOP AND PREDICT**

Will Miguel get to go along? Explain why or why not.

..............................................................................................................

..............................................................................................................

..............................................................................................................

**STOP AND PREDICT**

Then the sheep are brought in from the pueblo land of the Indians, from the big <u>mesa</u> where they have spent the winter. The sheep wagon is brought in too. Now the <u>flock</u> must stay close to the house so that everyone can help with the birth of the lambs.

At this time there is no question of who is Pedro and who is Gabriel and who am I.

**VOCABULARY**
**Fiesta de San Ysidro**—Spanish holiday.
**shearers**—people who clip the wool from sheep.
**mesa**—flat section on the top of a hill with cliff-like sides.
**flock**—group of animals that live and travel together.

Everyone helps without it making any difference who he is.

Even in the middle of the night someone can come into the bedroom where Faustina sleeps in one bed and me and Pedro in another. This one can say, "Come on, they need water."

There is no question who asks for the water or who goes to <u>fetch</u> it. We are quick to find our clothes and run to the spring, which is down the hill behind the tool shed. We

carry the water to where it is needed, to the lambing pens where the fires are kept going all night and the men must help the newest lambs who are having a hard time to get born. Or to the kitchen where my mother is always cooking, during this time, because someone is always eating.

**VOCABULARY**
**fetch**—go get something.

The lambs come at all different hours, and all our uncles and cousins stay at our house to be ready to help, and there is no breakfast time or dinner time or bed time. Everyone sleeps and eats when he can, no matter who he is, as long as he is ready when something is needed.

**STOP AND CLARIFY**

Why is Miguel so eager to be a helper?

.................................................................

.................................................................

.................................................................

**STOP AND CLARIFY**

I would like it to matter who he is, especially if it's me, Miguel. But that has never happened.

"Behind the tractor," my father will talk to me without even turning around, "in the tool shed there on the shelf is the <u>liniment</u>. The brown bottle. Hurry!"

My father will be busy bending over a <u>ewe</u> who tries hard to give birth to a lamb, working together with Uncle Eli. He will not even look up when I bring the medicine and put it into his hand.

**VOCABULARY**
**liniment**—medicine rubbed into the skin to relieve pain.
**ewe**—female sheep.

**"Sangre de Cristo Mountains"** continued

Once I tried to make my father see who I am. When he asked for some <u>burlap</u> bags to wrap one small lamb who was cold, I brought him the bags. When he took them from me, I said, "Here are the bags."

My father said nothing. He rubbed the lamb and wrapped it up.

"All right?" I said. "Okay?"

My father felt the neck of the lamb. "He'll be all right. It'll live."

**STOP AND QUESTION**

**QUESTION**

What does Miguel want his father to notice?

............................................................................

............................................................................

............................................................................

**STOP AND QUESTION**

"No," I shook my head. "I ask about the bags."

"What about the bags?"

"Are they all right?"

"What can be wrong with bags?"

"Wrong? Nothing. Except sometimes—." This was not what I wanted to talk about at all. "There can be holes in them."

"For our purpose, to wrap up new lambs, holes make no difference. That's why we use old bags."

**VOCABULARY**
**burlap**—strong woven cloth.

I knew all this. But I couldn't stop him from saying it.

"If we wanted to put something into them, like grain or wool, then we use new bags without holes." My father stood up now, looking down at me. "You didn't bring me any of the new wool bags, those that are in the corner of the shearing shed?"

"Me?" I said quickly. "Not me!" This is why it is hard for me to be Miguel sometimes, getting people to understand.

## STOP AND SUMMARIZE

What does Miguel want people to understand?

........................................................................................................

........................................................................................................

........................................................................................................

........................................................................................................

........................................................................................................

........................................................................................................

## GATHER YOUR THOUGHTS

**A. BRAINSTORM** "Sangre de Cristo Mountains" tells about an important time for Miguel and his family. Think about some important experiences that have happened to you and your family.

**1.** Write the name of your family in the center of the web.

**2.** Then brainstorm 4 or 5 things that have happened.

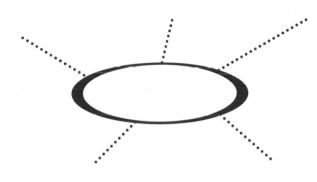

**B. NARROW THE TOPIC** Get ready to write an autobiographical paragraph about an important experience that happened to you and your family.

**1.** First look at the example on the left.

**2.** Then narrow your own topic the same way.

EXAMPLE

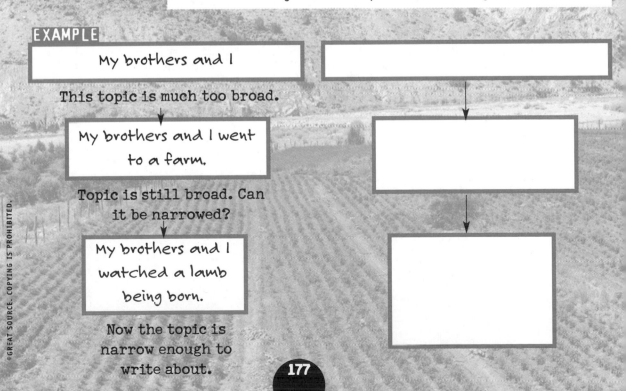

My brothers and I

This topic is much too broad.

My brothers and I went to a farm.

Topic is still broad. Can it be narrowed?

My brothers and I watched a lamb being born.

Now the topic is narrow enough to write about.

**C. GATHER DETAILS** Now write details about your narrowed topic. Use this "story star" to help organize the story you are going to tell.

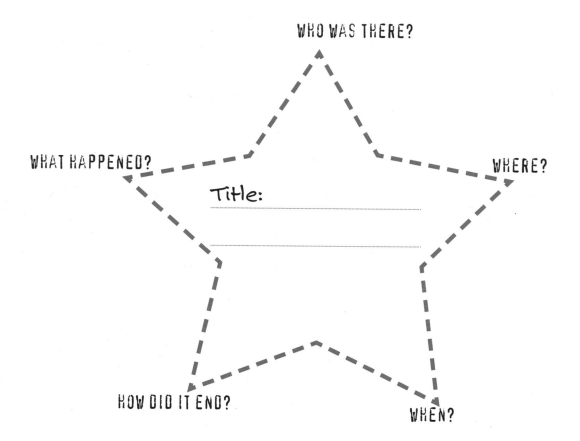

WHO WAS THERE?

WHAT HAPPENED?

WHERE?

Title: _____

_____

HOW DID IT END?

WHEN?

## IV. WRITE

Now write an **autobiographical paragraph.**

**1.** Stay focused on your narrowed topic and explain the points of your star.

**2.** Use the Writers' Checklist to help you revise.

### WRITERS' CHECKLIST

#### USAGE

☐ Did you use *to* to mean "in the direction of," *too* to mean "also" or "very," and *two* to mean the number?

EXAMPLES: *The two of us wanted to go to Dallas with my brother. We said, "Take us, too!"*

☐ Did you use *affect* as a verb to mean "to influence" and *effect* to mean "the result"?

EXAMPLES: *The lamb's bleating affected the herd. The effect was a group of very nervous animals.*

# V. WRAP-UP

What did Krumgold's story about Miguel make you think about?

**READERS'
CHECKLIST**

**DEPTH**

☐ Did the reading make you think about things?

☐ Did it set off thoughts beyond the surface topic?

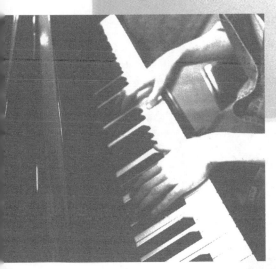

# Finding an Identity

Have you ever been the new kid in class? Have you ever had trouble making friends or felt left out of a group? In these sorts of situations, it can be tough to be confident about who you are and how you feel.

# 19: Bradley Chalkers

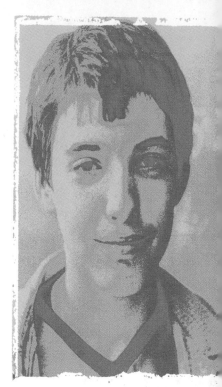

What's the easiest way to make a friend? The character in this next story has no friends, but he desperately needs them. What advice do you have?

## BEFORE YOU READ

Sometimes a word or idea is very important to a story. Creating a web can help you better understand what the word or idea means.

1. With a partner, discuss the word *friendship*. What does it mean to you? What does it mean to your partner?
2. Write your ideas on the Word Web.
3. List words, phrases, or situations that you think of when you hear the word *friendship*.

## Word Web

friendship

## II. READ

Now read "Bradley Chalkers."

**1.** Look for information that tells you more about the character of Bradley Chalkers.

**2.** In the Response Notes, write your **reactions** to Bradley.

**Response Notes**

### "Bradley Chalkers" from *There's a Boy in the Girls' Bathroom* by Louis Sachar

Bradley Chalkers sat at his desk in the back of the room—last seat, last row. No one sat at the desk next to him or at the one in front of him. He was an island.

If he could have, he would have sat in the closet. Then he could shut the door so he wouldn't have to listen to Mrs. Ebbel. He didn't think she'd mind. She'd probably like it better that way too. So would the rest of the class. All in all, he thought everyone would be much happier if he sat in the closet, but, unfortunately, his desk didn't fit.

"Class," said Mrs. Ebbel. "I would like you all to meet Jeff Fishkin. Jeff has just moved here from Washington, D.C., which, as you know, is our nation's capital."

EXAMPLE:
Sounds like he could be lonely.

## stop+retell

What have you learned about Bradley so far?

........................................................................

........................................................................

........................................................................

stop+retell

Bradley looked up at the new kid who was standing at the front of the room next to Mrs. Ebbel.

"Why don't you tell the class a little bit about yourself, Jeff," urged Mrs. Ebbel.

The new kid shrugged.

"There's no reason to be shy," said Mrs. Ebbel.

The new kid <u>mumbled</u> something, but Bradley couldn't hear what it was.

"Have you ever been to the White House, Jeff?" Mrs. Ebbel asked. "I'm sure the class would be very interested to hear about that."

"No, I've never been there," the new kid said very quickly as he shook his head.

Mrs. Ebbel smiled at him. "Well, I guess we'd better find you a place to sit." She looked around the room. "Hmm, I don't see anyplace except, I suppose you can sit there, at the back."

"No, not next to Bradley!" a girl in the front row exclaimed.

"At least it's better than *in front* of Bradley," said the boy next to her.

Mrs. Ebbel frowned. She turned to Jeff. "I'm sorry, but there are no other empty desks."

"I don't mind where I sit," Jeff mumbled.

"Well, nobody likes sitting . . . there," said Mrs. Ebbel.

"That's right," Bradley spoke up. "Nobody likes sitting next to me!" He smiled a strange

**VOCABULARY**

**mumbled**—said unclearly.

"**Bradley Chalkers**" continued

smile. He stretched his mouth so wide, it was hard to tell whether it was a smile or a frown.

## stop+retell

What do Bradley's classmates think of him?

......................................................................

......................................................................

......................................................................

......................................................................

## stop+retell

He stared at Jeff with <u>bulging</u> eyes as Jeff awkwardly sat down next to him. Jeff smiled back at him, so he looked away.

As Mrs. Ebbel began the lesson, Bradley took out a pencil and a piece of paper, and <u>scribbled</u>. He scribbled most of the morning, sometimes on the paper and sometimes on his desk. Sometimes he scribbled so hard his pencil point broke. Every time that happened he laughed. Then he'd tape the broken point to one of the <u>gobs</u> of junk in his desk, sharpen his pencil, and scribble again.

His desk was full of little wads of torn paper, pencil points, chewed erasers, and other unrecognizable stuff, all taped together.

Mrs. Ebbel handed back a language test. "Most of you did very well," she said. "I was very pleased. There were fourteen A's and the rest B's. Of course, there was one F, but . . ." She shrugged her shoulders.

### VOCABULARY
**bulging**—big and sticking out.
**scribbled**—wrote in a messy way.
**gobs**—large amounts.

**"Bradley Chalkers"** continued

Bradley held up his test for everyone to see and smiled that same <u>distorted</u> smile.

As Mrs. Ebbel went over the correct answers with the class, Bradley took out his pair of scissors and very carefully cut his test paper into tiny squares.

When the bell rang for recess, he put on his red jacket and walked outside, alone.

"Hey, Bradley, wait up!" somebody called after him.

Startled, he turned around.

Jeff, the new kid, hurried alongside him. "Hi," said Jeff.

Bradley stared at him in amazement.

Jeff smiled. "I don't mind sitting next to you," he said. "Really."

Bradley didn't know what to say.

"I have been to the White House," Jeff admitted. "If you want, I'll tell you about it."

Bradley thought a moment, then said, "Give me a dollar or I'll spit on you."

**VOCABULARY**
distorted—twisted.

# stop+retell

What have you learned about Bradley?

..................................................................................................

..................................................................................................

..................................................................................................

..................................................................................................

..................................................................................................

# III. GATHER YOUR THOUGHTS

**A. SHAPE AN OPINION** An opinion is a person's thought or belief. A fact is something that can be proven true or false.

**1.** Form an opinion about how Jeff Fishkin should react to Bradley Chalkers. You'll use your opinion in a persuasive paragraph.

**2.** Circle the opinion you like best or write an opinion of your own.

> **I think Jeff should keep trying to be friends with Bradley.**

> **I think Jeff should start ignoring Bradley like the other kids do.**

**Other:** I think Jeff should

_____

_____

**B. SUPPORT AN OPINION** Writers need to support their opinions with facts, examples, and experiences. In the chart below, write your opinion and then 3 pieces of support for it.

> OPINION

| SUPPORT #1 | SUPPORT #2 | SUPPORT #3 |
|------------|------------|------------|
|            |            |            |

# IV. WRITE

Now write a **persuasive paragraph** about what Jeff should do.

**1.** Open with your opinion statement and support it with details from your organizer.

**2.** End with a closing sentence that restates how you feel.

**3.** Use the Writers' Checklist to revise.

# V. WRAP-UP

How did the reading about Bradley Chalkers affect you?

Have you ever looked ahead in a book to see how long it is or what it's about? That's a way of skimming. Good readers skim first and read second. Doing this helps them know what to expect.

## BEFORE YOU READ

Skim through the selection "Sam Gribley."

**1.** Underline the 2 most important words in each line of the first paragraph.

**2.** Then glance quickly at the other paragraphs.

**3.** Answer the questions on the chart below.

## Skimming

| WHO'S FRIGHTFUL? |
| --- |
| |

| WHAT'S THIS STORY ABOUT? |
| --- |
| |

| HOW WOULD YOU DESCRIBE HER? |
| --- |
| |

| WHAT DO YOU THINK MIGHT HAPPEN TO SAM AND FRIGHTFUL? |
| --- |
| |

## READ

Now read "Sam Gribley."

**1.** As you read, think about the author's use of descriptive words.

**2.** Write any **questions** you have about the animals described.

### "Sam Gribley" from *On the Far Side of the Mountain* by Jean Craighead George

As a hot dry wind clears the air, I can see Frightful, my <u>peregrine falcon</u>, sitting in front of the six-foot-in-diameter <u>hemlock tree</u> that I <u>hollowed</u> out for a home. Unlike the chairs and people, Frightful has not changed. She still holds her body straight up and down and her head high in the manner of the peregrine falcon. Her <u>tawny</u> breast is decorated with black marks; her back is gray blue; her head black. When she flies, she is still a <u>crossbow</u> in the sky, and she still "waits on" above my head until I kick up a <u>pheasant</u> or a rabbit. Then she stoops, speeding toward her prey at two hundred miles an hour, the fastest animal on earth. She almost never misses.

"Hello, Frightful," I say.

"Creee, creee, creee, car-reet," she answers. That is her name for me, "Creee, creee, creee, car-reet." All peregrine falcons call the high-pitched creees, but when Frightful sees me in

EXAMPLE:
How old is the bird?

**VOCABULARY**

**peregrine falcon**—large, powerful bird with gray and white feathers, once used for hunting.
**hemlock tree**—kind of evergreen tree.
**hollowed**—cleared out to leave a gap or hole.
**tawny**—brownish-orange.
**crossbow**—weapon for shooting arrows.
**pheasant**—large bird with a long tail.

the morning or when I return from the forest, even when she is flying high above my head, she adds "car-reet." "Hello, Sam," she is saying.

She is perched on a T-block that I covered with <u>deerhide</u> to protect her feet. She lifts a broad foot and scratches her head with a curved claw on the end of a long, narrow toe.

"Creee, creee, creee, car-reet."

I call her name in her own language; I whistle three notes—low, high, low. She responds by lifting the feathers on her body, then shaking them. This is called *rousing*, which is feather talk meaning "I like you." I can't speak in feathers so I answer by <u>imitating</u> her love notes. I do this by pulling air through my two front teeth to make a soft, cozy sound.

# stop+organize

What have you learned about the two characters?

| SAM | FRIGHTFUL |
|---|---|
|  |  |

Sometimes I have nightmares that she has left me. I awake in a sweat and try to reason with myself. Frightful will not leave me, I say. If she were going to do that, she would have departed last spring when I was flying her free. A wild tercel, the male peregrine falcon,

**VOCABULARY**
**deerhide**—the skin of a deer.
**imitating**—copying.

**"Sam Gribley"** continued

passed overhead. The last of the vanishing eastern peregrine falcons breed in Greenland and Canada, and a few winter as far south as the Catskills. This one was on his way to his home in the north. Frightful playfully joined him. Together they performed the peregrine courtship dance, swooping low, zooming high, then spiraling earthward. I was scared. I thought Frightful was going to leave me. I whistled. She instantly pulled deeply on her wings and sped back. Within a few feet of my outstretched hand, she braked and <u>alighted</u> on my glove as softly as the fluff from a dandelion seed. "Creee, creee, creee, car-reet," she said. "Hello, Frightful," I answered happily.

Now, I whistle her name again. She turns her head and looks at me. Her curved, flesh-ripping beak looks sweet and <u>demure</u> when you see her head on. Her overhanging brow shades large black eyes that are outlined in white feathers. She is a gorgeous creature.

At peace with me and herself, she bobs her head as she follows the flight of a bird. I cannot see it, but I know it's a bird because Frightful's feathers tell me so. She has flattened most of them to her body while lifting those between her shoulders. "Bird," that means. "Human" is feathers fluttened, eyes wide, neck pulled in, wings drooped to fly.

I get to my feet. I have daydreamed enough. While the last of the <u>haze</u> burns off, I <u>weed</u> the

### VOCABULARY
**alighted**—came down and settled gently.
**demure**—shy.
**haze**—early morning cloudiness.
**weed**—pull out unwanted plants.

meadow garden and split kindling before returning to my tree.

A hot sun now filters down through the lacy needles of the hemlocks in my grove. I look for Alice, wondering what she's up to.

## stop+organize

What 2 things have happened in the story so far?

**1.**

**2.**

stop+organize

That's how one thinks of Alice—what is she up to? She's probably gone downmountain to the farm to see that pig she talks to.

Sticks snap in the distance. Someone is coming. Frightful has clamped her feathers to her body to say that whoever it is is not a friend. Her feathers read "danger." The phoebe clicks out his alarm cry and I tense. I have learned to heed these warning signals. The birds and animals see, hear, smell, and feel approaching danger long before I do. I press my ear to the ground and hear footsteps. They are heavy: possibly a black bear.

I smell the musky scent of warning from my friend Baron Weasel. The Baron, who was

### VOCABULARY
**meadow**—grassy area.
**kindling**—wood used to start a fire.
**filters**—passes slowly.
**grove**—small area with trees.
**heed**—listen to; pay close attention to.
**musky**—strong-smelling.

**"Sam Gribley"** continued

living here when I arrived, considers himself the real owner of the mountaintop, but because he finds me interesting, he lets me stay.

## stop+organize

What are 2 things have you learned about Sam Gribley?

1.

2.

Right now he doesn't like what's coming and dives into his den under the boulder. I glance at Frightful again.

Her feathers are flattened to her body, her eyes wide, neck stretched, and her wings are lowered for flight. "Human," she is saying. I wait.

A man in a green uniform rounds the bend, sees me, and <u>hesitates</u> as if uncertain.

"Hello," I say aloud, and to myself: Here it comes. He's some official. I've got to go to school this fall. Dad didn't pay the taxes on the farm. Alice is up to something again.

"Do you know where Sam Gribley lives?" he asks.

"Here," I answer. "I'm Sam Gribley."

"Oh," he says and glances at my face, then my berry-dyed T-shirt, and finally, my moccasins. These seem to confuse him. Apparently he is not expecting a teenager.

**VOCABULARY**
**hesitates**—pauses; delays.

# stop+organize

Who has arrived? What do you think will happen?

stop+organize

**Response Notes**

## "Sam Gribley" continued

Suddenly he looks over my shoulder and walks past me. I spin around to see him standing before Frightful.

"My name is Leon Longbridge," he says with his back to me. "I'm the conservation officer. You're <u>harboring</u> an <u>endangered</u> species—a peregrine falcon."

I am unable to speak.

"Keeping an endangered species carries a fine and a year's imprisonment."

"I didn't know that." He faces me.

"You should have, but since you didn't, I won't arrest you. But I will have to <u>confiscate</u> the bird."

I can't believe what I am hearing.

# stop+organize

What problem does Sam face? How do you think Sam will solve it?

stop+organize

**VOCABULARY**
**harboring**—sheltering.
**endangered**—threatened; nearly extinct.
**confiscate**—take away.

# III. GATHER YOUR THOUGHTS

**A. ANALYZE SENSORY WORDS** Organize the descriptive words below from Jean Craighead George's story about Sam Gribley.

**1.** Put each of the words in one of 3 categories.

**2.** Then name each category.

| | | | |
|---|---|---|---|
| tawny | high | heavy | cozy |
| high-pitched | flattened | musky | flesh-ripping |
| hot | wild | demure | white |
| soft | tense | gorgeous | endangered |

**B. BRAINSTORM SENSORY DETAILS** Get ready to write a descriptive paragraph about an animal that is special to you.

**1.** Build a word bank you could use to describe your animal.

**2.** Think of at least 2 words for each of the 5 senses.

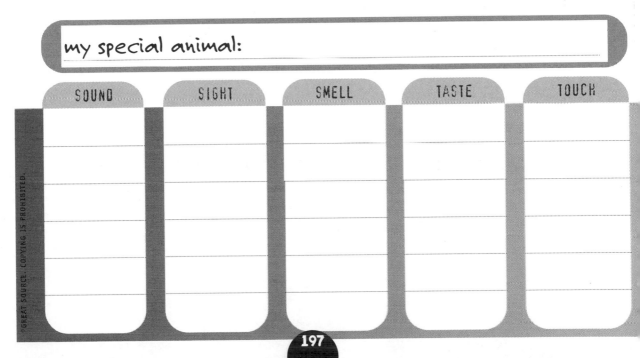

my special animal:

| SOUND | SIGHT | SMELL | TASTE | TOUCH |
|---|---|---|---|---|
| | | | | |

**C. CREATE A DESCRIPTION** Write sentences that describe your animal.
1. Write 5 of your sensory words in the small boxes below on the left.
2. On the right, write a sentence that uses the sensory word. An example is done for you.

EXAMPLE:

fluffy

Ex, my new puppy, is my fluffy, furry pillow.

SIGHT word

TOUCH word

SMELL word

SOUND word

TASTE word

## WRITE

Now write a **descriptive paragraph.**

1. Start with a topic sentence that tells how you feel about your animal.
2. Then use your sentences from page 198 to describe the animal.
3. Use the Writers' Checklist to help you revise.

### WRITERS' CHECKLIST

#### USAGE

☐ Did you use *good* as an adjective and *well* as an adverb? EXAMPLES: The horse was a *good* jumper. The horse jumped *well*.

☐ Did you use *bad* as an adjective and *badly* as an adverb? EXAMPLES: My rabbit's *bad* leg hurt him. It was cut *badly*.

# V. WRAP-UP

## What is "Sam Gribley" all about?

# Native Americans

The first white people came to the land we now call America about 500 years ago. Native Americans had already been living here for more than 15,000 years. They had established tribes and ways of life. How much do we really know about the history, culture, and beliefs of Native Americans?

How would you prove yourself? How will you show you've grown up? What will that moment be like? Luther Standing Bear, at age eight, proved himself during a buffalo hunt with his father, a Lakota chief.

## I. BEFORE YOU READ

What do you know about buffalo and how they were hunted? To get started, complete the K-W-L Chart below.

1. Write what you know about buffalo hunts in the **K** column.
2. Write what you want to learn in the **W** column. Save the **L** column for later.

**K-W-L CHART**

| **K** What I **K**now | **W** What I **W**ant to Know | **L** What I **L**earned |
|---|---|---|
| | | |

## II. READ

Now read part of Luther Standing Bear's autobiography.

**1.** As you read, **mark** or **highlight** key events in the beginning, middle, and end of his story.

**2.** Use the Response Notes to jot information that helps answer questions in the K-W-L Chart.

---

### "Buffalo Hunt" from *My Indian Boyhood* by Luther Standing Bear

**RESPONSE NOTES**

The next morning the hunters were catching their horses about daybreak. I arose with my father and went out and caught my pony. I wanted to do whatever he did and show him that he did not have to tell me what to do. We brought our animals to the tipi and got our bows and arrows and mounted. From over the village came the hunters. Most of them were leading their running horses. These running horses were anxious for the hunt and came prancing, their ears straight up and their tails waving in the air. We were joined with perhaps a hundred or more riders, some of whom carried bows and arrows and some armed with guns.

EXAMPLE:
Hunters used guns
and bows and
arrows.

The buffalo were reported to be about five or six miles away as we should count distance now. At that time we did not measure distance in miles. One camping distance was about ten miles, and these buffalo were said to be about one half camping distance away.

**VOCABULARY**

**tipi**—tent made of hides stitched together, used by Native Americans of the Great Plains.

**RESPONSE NOTES**

Some of the horses were to be left at a stopping place just before the herd was reached. These horses were pack animals which were taken along to carry extra blankets or weapons. They were trained to remain there until the hunters came for them. Though they were neither <u>hobbled</u> nor tied, they stood still during the shooting and noise of the chase.

My pony was a black one and a good runner. I felt very important as I rode along with the hunters and my father, the chief. I kept as close to him as I could.

**STOP AND THINK**

What scene or setting has Standing Bear described?

............................................................................

............................................................................

............................................................................

............................................................................

............................................................................

**STOP AND THINK**

Two men had been chosen to <u>scout</u> or to lead the party. These two men were in a sense policemen whose work it was to keep order. They carried large sticks of ash wood, something like a policeman's <u>billy</u>, though

**VOCABULARY**
**hobbled**—with legs fastened together.
**scout**—go out to observe or get information.
**billy**—club or nightstick.

**"Buffalo Hunt"** continued

longer. They rode ahead of the party while the rest of us kept in a group close together. The leaders went ahead until they sighted the herd of grazing buffalo. Then they stopped and waited for the rest of us to ride up. We all rode slowly toward the herd, which on sight of us had come together, although they had been scattered here and there over the plain. When they saw us, they all ran close together as if at the command of a leader. We continued riding slowly toward the herd until one of the leaders shouted, "Ho-ka-he!" which means, "Ready, Go!" At that command every man started for the herd. I had been listening, too, and the minute the hunters started, I started also.

Away I went, my little pony putting all he had into the race. It was not long before I lost sight of father, but I kept going just the same. I threw my blanket back and the chill of the autumn morning struck my body, but I did not mind. On I went. It was wonderful to race over the ground with all these horsemen about me. There was no shouting, no noise of any kind except the pounding of the horses' feet. The herd was now running and had raised a cloud of dust. I felt no fear until we had entered this cloud of dust and I could see nothing about me—only hear the sound of feet. Where was father? Where was I going? On I rode through the cloud, for I knew I must keep going.

## How does Standing Bear feel as the hunt begins?

### RESPONSE NOTES

Then all at once I realized that I was in the midst of the buffalo, their dark bodies rushing all about me and their great heads moving up and down to the sound of their hoofs beating upon the earth. Then it was that fear overcame me and I leaned close down upon my little pony's body and <u>clutched</u> him tightly. I can never tell you how I felt toward my pony at that moment. All thought of shooting had left my mind. I was seized by blank fear. In a moment or so, however, my senses became clearer, and I could <u>distinguish</u> other sounds beside the clatter of feet. I could hear a shot now and then and I could see the buffalo beginning to break up into small bunches. I could not see father nor any of my <u>companions</u> yet, but my fear was vanishing and I was safe. I let my pony run. The buffalo looked too large for me to tackle, anyway, so I just kept going. Pretty soon I saw a young calf that looked

### VOCABULARY
**clutched**—held tightly.
**distinguish**—identify.
**companions**—persons who go along with or who share what another is doing.

**"Buffalo Hunt"** continued

about my size. I remembered now what father had told me the night before as we sat about the fire. Those instructions were important for me now to follow.

**STOP AND THINK**

Why does Standing Bear feel less afraid now?

I was still back of the calf, being unable to get alongside of him. I was <u>anxious</u> to get a shot, yet afraid to try, as I was still very nervous. While my pony was making all speed to come alongside, I chanced a shot and to my surprise my arrow landed. My second arrow <u>glanced</u> along the back of the animal and sped on between the horns, making only a slight wound. My third arrow hit a spot that

**VOCABULARY**
**anxious**—uneasy; worried about what might happen.
**glanced**—hit and went off at a slant.

made the running beast slow up in his gait. I shot a fourth arrow, and though it, too, landed it was not a fatal wound. It seemed to me that it was taking a lot of shots, and I was not proud of my marksmanship. I was glad, however, to see the animal going slower and I knew that one more shot would make me a hunter. My horse seemed to know his own importance. His two ears stood straight forward and it was not necessary for me to urge him to get closer to the buffalo. I was soon by the side of the buffalo and one more shot brought the chase to a close. I jumped from my pony, and as I stood by my fallen game, I looked all around wishing that the world could see. But I was alone. In my determination to stay by until I had won my buffalo, I had not noticed that I was far from every one else. No admiring friends were about, and as far as I could see I was on the plain alone. The herd of buffalo had completely disappeared. And as for father, much as I wished for him, he was out of sight and I had no idea where he was.

**VOCABULARY**
**gait**—steps used in running.
**fatal**—causing death.
**marksmanship**—skill in shooting.
**game**—wild animals, birds or fish hunted or caught for sport or for food.
**plain**—flat stretch of land or prairie.

Why do you think Standing Bear makes a point to say "I was on the plain alone"?

Now go back to the K-W-L Chart on page 202 and record what you learned from "Buffalo Hunt."

**A. DEVELOP A TOPIC** Think about a time when you proved yourself. Then complete the web below.

WHY IT WAS IMPORTANT?

HOW I FELT?

WHAT I HAD TO DO?

Proving Myself

WHO WAS THERE?

WHEN IT HAPPENED?

WHERE IT HAPPENED?

**B. ORGANIZE A STORY** To write a personal narrative, you need a beginning, middle, and end to your story.
**1.** Think through the entire story you want to tell.
**2.** Then write in the storyboards what you will say at the beginning, middle, and end.

beginning

middle

end

# IV. WRITE

Write a **personal narrative** about a time you proved yourself.

**1.** Give your story a beginning, a middle, and an end.

**2.** Use the Writers' Checklist when you revise.

Continue your writing on the next page.

## WRITERS' CHECKLIST

### COMMA SPLICES

☐ Did you avoid writing comma splices? A comma splice occurs when two sentences are joined with only a comma. To fix a comma splice, you can add a conjunction (such as *and, or, but,* or *so*) before the comma. You may also replace the comma with a semicolon or create separate sentences.

EXAMPLES: *I took a deep breath, I was scared.* (comma splice) *I took a deep breath, and I was scared.* (correct) *I took a deep breath; I was scared.* (correct)

Continue your writing from the previous page.

_____

_____

_____

_____

_____

_____

_____

_____

_____

_____

_____

_____

## V. WRAP-UP

What did Luther Standing Bear's personal story make you think about?

_____

_____

_____

_____

_____

## 22: The Sunflower Room

Do you look at the posters or TV ads about upcoming movies? They get you interested in the movie and give you a sneak preview of what's to come. Pictures in books can also give you a glimpse of what's to come.

### BEFORE YOU READ

Take a picture walk through "The Sunflower Room."
1. Look carefully at all the pictures.
2. Read the captions. Choose 2 photos to write about.
3. Then make a prediction.

**PICTURE WALK**

THE PHOTO OF . . .          TELLS ME . . .

THE PHOTO OF . . .          REMINDS ME OF . . .

I think this story will be about . . .

## READ

Now read "The Sunflower Room."
**1. Clarify** the events of this story as you read.
**2.** Keep track of important details in the Response Notes.

**RESPONSE NOTES**

EXAMPLE:
Annie=sad
while waiting
for her uncle

**"The Sunflower Room"** from *Remember My Name* by Sara H. Banks

Annie sat on the cabin steps alone. Her long dark skirt was tucked around her knees as she chewed <u>absently</u> on the end of her <u>glossy</u> braid that was the dark brown of a horse chestnut. From the lilac bushes in the yard, a mockingbird sang a joyful song. She looked over at him and sighed deeply. He sounded much too happy for such a sad day.

It was September and the fields were still green. Down in the meadow, sunflowers grew tall, their bright yellow heads following the path to the sun. Annie was waiting for her uncle William Blackfeather. She wondered what he'd look like. Although he was a <u>full-blood</u>, like her mother, he might have changed since the last time she saw him. That had

**absently**—without paying attention.
**glossy**—shiny.
**full-blood**—100 percent (Cherokee Native American, in this case).

**Two Native American girls picking berries**

**"The Sunflower Room"** continued

been five years ago, when she was six years old. He was her mother's brother and lived at New Echota, the Cherokee capital of the Nation. Now he was coming to Star Mountain to take her back with him. And she wasn't at all sure that she wanted to go. In fact, she was pretty sure that she didn't. But no one had asked what she wanted.

"I still don't see why I have to go," she muttered to no one in particular. "I could stay here and live with *Nanye'hi*. She can teach me everything I need to know. I don't need to go to school."

STOP AND PREDICT

Will Annie be able to convince Nanye'hi to let her stay?

........................................................................

........................................................................

........................................................................

STOP AND PREDICT

Everything was wrong somehow. For a moment, the blackness that sometimes fell over her seemed about to happen. Her parents were . . . the word drifted in and she pushed it away. She couldn't even *think* the word. They were gone . . . but the word pushed its way into her head. They were dead. Something gripped her heart with a fierceness that made her catch her breath. They were gone. And she missed them so.

**VOCABULARY**
Cherokee—a particular Native American tribe.
gripped—took hold of.
fierceness—strong or extreme feeling.

A young girl in traditional Navajo dress

©GREAT SOURCE. COPYING IS PROHIBITED.

A soft footfall sounded behind her and she turned. Her grandmother, *Nanye'hi*, stood in the doorway.

"It's time, little one," she said, holding out her hand. "Your uncle will be here soon."

*Nanye'hi* was tall and thin and wore the traditional Indian dress of a <u>buckskin</u> <u>shift</u> and soft boots. Her hair, sprinkled with gray, was worn in two long braids. Taking her grandmother's hand, Annie asked, "How do you know? How do you know he's coming now?"

"The mockingbird, *Conconolatally*, told me with one of his four hundred tongues," replied *Nanye'hi*. "Come now, *Agin'agili*," she said, using Annie's Cherokee name. "You must be ready when my son William comes to fetch you."

**STOP AND CLARIFY**

Why is Annie unhappy about leaving?

........................................................................

........................................................................

........................................................................

**STOP AND CLARIFY**

**VOCABULARY**

**buckskin**—soft, strong, yellow leather made from the skins of deer or sheep.

**shift**—loosely fitting dress.

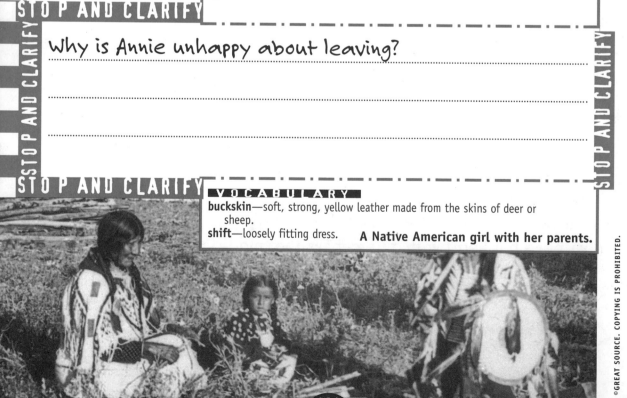

**A Native American girl with her parents.**

**"The Sunflower Room"** continued

"We must use my other name," whispered Annie. But her grandmother paid no attention to her. "Come," she said.

When she was six, Annie had discovered a place where sunflowers grew in a kind of natural square, the bright yellow blossoms always turning towards the sun. Taller than her head, the stalks had offered shade on a hot afternoon when she'd been waiting for her mother, who was picking blackberries in the sunlit field. Hot and sleepy, Annie had wandered off into the cool green shelter of the flowers.

Hours later, Annie was found asleep in what soon became her favorite place. Each year after that, Annie's father had planted sunflowers so that they grew in a square, and when they were higher than her head, her mother had woven leaves and branches through them, making a small room, a private place just for Annie. The day before yesterday, Annie had gone down to the meadow, to her secret place.

**STOP AND RETELL**

How would you describe Annie's secret place?

Slipping through the narrow opening in the wall of green, she had entered her sunflower room. From the deep pocket of her shift, she took out her favorite doll and laid it gently on the ground. The doll's <u>features</u>, once brightly painted, were blurred and <u>faint</u> from much loving. Her dress of deerskin was worn soft as silk and the feather in her hair was <u>bedraggled</u> and <u>wispy</u>.

Reaching up, Annie tore off a <u>broad</u> leaf from a sunflower stalk and wrapped it around her doll like a shawl. Then, with a sharp stick, she began digging a hole. When she'd finished, she laid the doll inside and covered her with earth.

"I'm too old for you now," she said softly. "And now you are buried here with my name. Where I am going, I will be called Annie Stuart. No one will remember my Cherokee name."

## STOP AND QUESTION

What does it mean that Annie buried her doll and her name?

................................................................

................................................................

................................................................

................................................................

................................................................

## VOCABULARY

**features**—parts of the face.
**faint**—light; hard to see.
**bedraggled**—wet and limp, as if having been dragged through the mud.
**wispy**—thin; fragile.
**broad**—wide.

**"The Sunflower Room"** continued

The world she was entering would be a different world from the one she had known on Star Mountain. No one had told her this, but she knew, just the same. Nothing would ever be the same again.

And so, *Agin'agili* buried her doll along with her name and turned her back on her secret place.

**STOP AND RETELL    STOP AND RETELL    STOP AND RETELL**

Go back over the story. Retell the main events in the boxes below.

1.

2.

3.

4.

5.

6.

**A Native American family seated in front of a tipi**

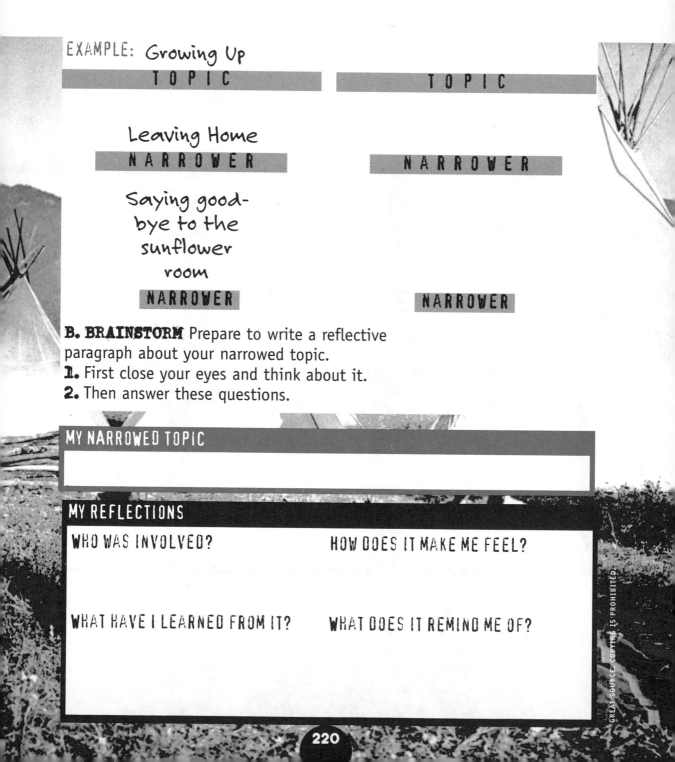

## III GATHER YOUR THOUGHTS

**A. NARROW YOUR FOCUS** Writers narrow their focus by beginning with a large topic and dividing it into smaller subtopics.

**1.** Choose one of these 4 large topics: My Family, School Days, Growing Up, Friends. Write it below.

**2.** Use the organizer to narrow the topic. Look at the example for ideas.

EXAMPLE: Growing Up

| TOPIC | TOPIC |
|---|---|
| Leaving Home | |
| **NARROWER** | **NARROWER** |
| Saying good-bye to the sunflower room | |
| **NARROWER** | **NARROWER** |

**B. BRAINSTORM** Prepare to write a reflective paragraph about your narrowed topic.

**1.** First close your eyes and think about it.

**2.** Then answer these questions.

### MY NARROWED TOPIC

### MY REFLECTIONS

WHO WAS INVOLVED?                HOW DOES IT MAKE ME FEEL?

WHAT HAVE I LEARNED FROM IT?      WHAT DOES IT REMIND ME OF?

# IV. WRITE

Write a **reflective paragraph** about your topic.

**1.** Open with a topic sentence that tells how you feel about the topic. Give details from your organizer on the previous page.

**2.** Use the Writers' Checklist to help you revise.

## WRITERS' CHECKLIST

### SUBJECT/VERB AGREEMENT

☐ Did you use singular verbs with singular subjects? *Everybody, everyone, nobody,* and *no one* are all singular. When one of these words is the subject of a sentence, the verb in the sentence must also be singular. EXAMPLES: *Everyone is (not are) here. No one has (not have) been there.*

## What did "The Sunflower Room" mean to you?

Norton Juster's most famous work, *The Phantom Tollbooth*, tells of a hard-to-please boy's fantastic journey. The boy travels through a world where nothing is as it seems, and the only way to avoid danger is by using his brain.

THE PHANTOM TOLLBOOTH

NORTON JUSTER

Illustrations by JULES FEIFFER

Do you ever feel bored? The next story is about a young boy, Milo, who feels bored every minute of every day. Writers explore interesting characters to help us know and understand more about ourselves.

## I. BEFORE YOU READ

Read the first 3 paragraphs of "Milo" on the next page.
**1.** Think about what being bored feels like.
**2.** Answer the questions about boredom below.

## Web

HOW DOES IT END?

WHAT IS IT LIKE?

Boredom

HOW DOES IT FEEL?

WHERE DOES IT HAPPEN?

WHEN DOES IT HAPPEN?

## II. READ

Now read "Milo."

**1.** As you are reading, think about Milo and what happens to him.

**2.** Write your **predictions** in the Response Notes.

### "Milo" from *The Phantom Tollbooth*
### by Norton Juster

There was once a boy named Milo who didn't know what to do with himself—not just sometimes, but always.

When he was in school he longed to be out, and when he was out he longed to be in. On the way he thought about coming home, and coming home he thought about going. Wherever he was he wished he were somewhere else, and when he got there he wondered why he'd bothered. Nothing really interested him—least of all the things that should have.

"It seems to me that almost everything is a waste of time," he remarked one day as he walked <u>dejectedly</u> home from school. "I can't see the point in learning to solve useless problems, or subtracting turnips from turnips, or knowing where <u>Ethiopia</u> is or how to spell February." And, since no one bothered to explain otherwise, he regarded the process of <u>seeking</u> knowledge as the greatest waste of time of all.

EXAMPLE:
Milo might discover something he needs to know.

**VOCABULARY**
**dejectedly**—feeling depressed and gloomy.
**Ethiopia**—a country in northeast Africa.
**seeking**—searching for.

As he and his unhappy thoughts hurried along (for while he was never <u>anxious</u> to be where he was going, he liked to get there as quickly as possible) it seemed a great wonder that the world, which was so large, could sometimes feel so small and empty.

"And worst of all," he continued sadly, "there's nothing for me to do, nowhere I'd care to go, and hardly anything worth seeing." He <u>punctuated</u> this last thought with such a deep sigh that a house sparrow singing nearby stopped and rushed home to be with his family.

## Double-entry Journal

Read this quote from the story. Then write how it makes you feel.

| Quote | My thoughts |
|---|---|
| "And worst of all . . . there's nothing for me to do, nowhere I'd care to go, and hardly anything worth seeing.'" | |

Without stopping or looking up, Milo <u>dashed</u> past the buildings and busy shops that lined the street and in a few minutes reached home—dashed through the lobby—hopped onto the elevator—two, three, four, five, six,

**VOCABULARY**
anxious—eager; full of a strong desire.
punctuated—emphasized.
dashed—rushed.

**"Milo"** continued

seven, eight, and off again—opened the apartment door—rushed into his room— flopped <u>dejectedly</u> into a chair, and <u>grumbled</u> softly, "Another long afternoon."

He looked <u>glumly</u> at all the things he owned. The books that were too much trouble to read, the tools he'd never learned to use, the small electric automobile he hadn't driven in months—or was it years?—and the hundreds of other games and toys, and bats and balls, and bits and pieces scattered around him. And then, to one side of the room, just next to the <u>phonograph</u>, he noticed something he had certainly never seen before.

Who could possibly have left such an enormous package and such a strange one? For, while it was not quite square, it was definitely not round, and for its size it was larger than almost any other big package of smaller <u>dimension</u> that he'd ever seen.

## Double-entry Journal

Read this quote from the story. Then write your thoughts about it.

| Quote | My thoughts |
| --- | --- |
| "He looked glumly at all the things he owned." | |

**VOCABULARY**
**dejectedly**—with little or no hope.
**grumbled**—muttered; complained.
**glumly**—gloomily.
**phonograph**—record player.
**dimension**—size.

Attached to one side was a bright-blue envelope which said simply: "FOR MILO, WHO HAS PLENTY OF TIME."

Of course, if you've ever gotten a surprise package, you can imagine how puzzled and excited Milo was; and if you've never gotten one, pay close attention, because someday you might.

"I don't think it's my birthday," he <u>puzzled</u>, "and Christmas must be months away, and I haven't been outstandingly good, or even good at all." (He had to admit this even to himself.) "Most probably I won't like it anyway, but since I don't know where it came from, I can't possibly send it back." He thought about it for quite a while and then opened the envelope, but just to be polite.

## Double-entry Journal

Read and respond to the quote below.

| Quote | My thoughts |
|---|---|
| "Most probably I won't like it anyway, but since I don't know where it came from, I can't possibly send it back." | |

**V O C A B U L A R Y**
**puzzled**—thought confusedly.

## III. GATHER YOUR THOUGHTS

**A. UNDERSTAND A CHARACTER** Make notes about Milo below. In each of the ovals surrounding his name, write a word that describes him.

Milo

**B. DESCRIBE AN OPINION** Get ready to write a paragraph of opinion about Milo. List 2 things that Milo is like and 2 things he is not like.

1. Milo is like

2. He is also like

3. Milo is not like

4. He is also not like

**C. WRITE A TOPIC SENTENCE** Choose 3 words to finish this sentence about Milo. Use it as the topic sentence.

Milo is                              /                              /

and                                                                      .

# IV. WRITE

Write a **paragraph of opinion** about Milo.
1. Begin with your topic sentence.
2. Support your topic sentence with details.
3. Use the Writers' Checklist to help you revise.

# V. WRAP-UP

What did you enjoy best about "Milo"?

# 24: Milo continued

Would you go to look for buried treasure without a map? You probably wouldn't. You would first want to know where you are going. The same is true for reading. Before you start a story, ask yourself, "What is this about, and what's going to happen?"

## I. BEFORE YOU READ

Get ready to read the next part of the story of Milo.
**1.** Read the statements below.
**2.** Say whether you agree or disagree and then explain why.

| Anticipation Guide | (CIRCLE ONE) |
|---|---|
| Milo will open the package. | yes    no |
| Why? | |
| The package will make Milo a whole new person. | yes    no |
| Why? | |
| The package will hurt Milo. | yes    no |
| Why? | |
| Milo's mother will interrupt and take away the package. | yes    no |
| Why? | |

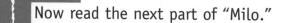

## II. READ

Now read the next part of "Milo."

**1.** As you are reading, **react** and **connect** to the action and characters.

**2.** Write your reactions in the Response Notes.

**Response Notes**

---

### "Milo" (continued) from
### *The Phantom Tollbooth* by Norton Juster

"ONE GENUINE TURNPIKE TOLLBOOTH," it stated—and then it went on:

"EASILY ASSEMBLED AT HOME, AND FOR USE BY THOSE WHO HAVE NEVER TRAVELED IN LANDS BEYOND."

"Beyond what?" thought Milo as he continued to read.

"THIS PACKAGE CONTAINS THE FOLLOWING ITEMS:

"One (1) genuine turnpike tollbooth to be erected according to directions.

"Three (3) precautionary signs to be used in a precautionary fashion.

"Assorted coins for use in paying tolls.

"One (1) map, up to date and carefully drawn by master cartographers, depicting natural and man-made features.

**EXAMPLE:**
This is so weird, very funny!

**VOCABULARY**
**TOLLBOOTH**—small building on a highway or road at which drivers pay money for using the roads.
**erected**—built; constructed.
**precautionary**—steps taken in advance to avoid danger or trouble.
**cartographers**—people who make maps.
**depicting**—showing.

**"Milo"** continued

"One (1) book of rules and traffic <u>regulations</u>, which may not be bent or broken."

And in smaller letters at the bottom it concluded:

"RESULTS ARE NOT GUARANTEED, BUT IF NOT PERFECTLY SATISFIED, YOUR WASTED TIME WILL BE REFUNDED."

Following the instructions, which told him to cut here, lift there, and fold back all around, he soon had the tollbooth unpacked and set up on its stand. He fitted the windows in place and attached the roof, which extended out on both sides, and fastened on the coin box. It was very much like the tollbooths he'd seen many times on family trips, except of course it was much smaller and purple.

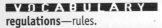

What do you think Milo will do with the tollbooth?

.................................................................................

.................................................................................

.................................................................................

.................................................................................

**VOCABULARY**
**regulations**—rules.

"What a strange present," he thought to himself. "The least they could have done was to send a highway with it, for it's terribly impractical without one." But since, at the time, there was nothing else he wanted to play with, he set up three signs,

SLOW DOWN APPROACHING TOLLBOOTH

PLEASE HAVE YOUR FARE READY

HAVE YOUR DESTINATION IN MIND

and slowly unfolded the map.

As the announcement stated, it was a beautiful map, in many colors, showing principal roads, rivers and seas, towns and cities, mountains and valleys, intersections and detours, and sites of outstanding interest both beautiful and historic.

The only trouble was that Milo had never heard of any of the places it indicated, and even the names sounded most peculiar.

## stop+predict

What will Milo do with his map and tollbooth?

....................................................................................

....................................................................................

....................................................................................

....................................................................................

....................................................................................

stop+predict

**VOCABULARY**
**impractical**—not useful.
**FARE**—money to pay the toll.
**principal**—main.

**"Milo"** continued

"I don't think there really is such a country," he <u>concluded</u> after studying it carefully. "Well, it doesn't matter anyway." And he closed his eyes and poked a finger at the map.

"Dictionopolis," read Milo slowly when he saw what his finger had chosen. "Oh, well, I might as well go there as anywhere."

He walked across the room and dusted the car off carefully. Then, taking the map and rule book with him, he hopped in and, for lack of anything better to do, drove slowly up to the tollbooth. As he deposited his coin and rolled past he remarked <u>wistfully</u>, "I do hope this is an interesting game, otherwise the afternoon will be so terribly dull."

## stop+predict

What do you think will happen to Milo in Dictionopolis?

........................................................................................

........................................................................................

........................................................................................

........................................................................................

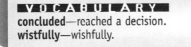

**VOCABULARY**
**concluded**—reached a decision.
**wistfully**—wishfully.

# III. GATHER YOUR THOUGHTS

**A. RESPOND** What is your reaction to Norton Juster's story? Circle all the words that apply.

"Milo" made me . . .

> laugh    cry    smile    cringe    sleepy    excited
> curious    bored    sad    happy    other _____

**B. CONNECT TO A CHARACTER** Now connect the stories to your own life. Complete these sentences.

Milo and I have these 2 things in common:

.........................................................................................................

.........................................................................................................

Milo and I are different in these 2 ways:

.........................................................................................................

.........................................................................................................

What I would have done with the tollbooth:

.........................................................................................................

.........................................................................................................

**C. DEVELOP A PARAGRAPH** Get ready to write a letter to Norton Juster.
**1.** Begin with an opinion statement that sums up your feelings about Juster's writing.
**2.** Then list 3 reasons that support your opinion.
**3.** End with a sentence that explains whether or not you'd like to read more of Juster's writing.

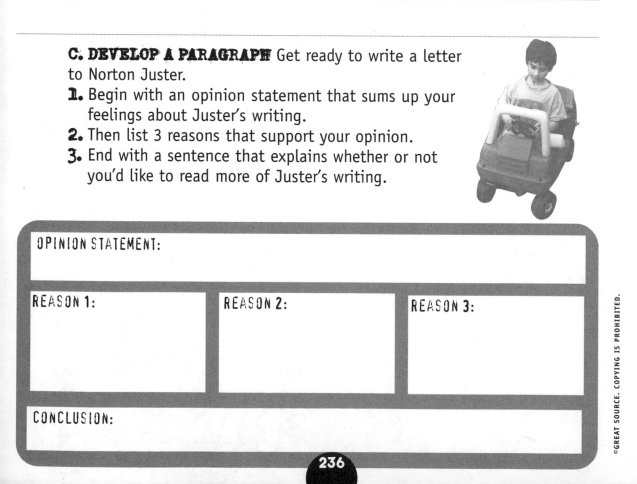

| OPINION STATEMENT: | | |
|---|---|---|
| REASON 1: | REASON 2: | REASON 3: |
| CONCLUSION: | | |

# IV. WRITE

Write a **letter** to Norton Juster.

**1.** Use your notes from the previous page to organize your letter into 3 basic parts.

**2.** Use the Writers' Checklist to help you revise.

date:

Dear Mr. Juster,

## WRITERS' CHECKLIST

### END PUNCTUATION

☐ Did you put a period at the end of sentences that make a statement or give an order? EXAMPLE: *I enjoyed The Phantom Tollbooth.*

☐ Did you put a question mark at the end of sentences that ask a question or make a request? EXAMPLE: *Have you read the book lately?*

☐ Did you use an exclamation mark with sentences that show strong emotions? EXAMPLE: *Milo is a funny kid!*

Continue your writing on the next page.

Continue your writing from the previous page.

_____

_____

_____

_____

_____

_____

_____

                                        Sincerely yours,

_____

V. **WRAP-UP**
What made Juster's writing easy or difficult for
you to read?

**READERS'
CHECKLIST**

**EASE**
☐ Was the passage
easy to read?
☐ Were you able to
read it smoothly
and without
difficulty?

_____

_____

_____

_____

_____

# Acknowledgments

**8** "Thinking," by Lorna Dee Cervantes is reprinted with permission from the publisher of "Kikirikí," edited by Sylvia Cavazos Peña (Houston: Arte Público Press: University of Houston, 1981).

**10** "I Belong," by A. Whiterock. American Indian Historical Society.

**13** "Father," from LIVING UP THE STREET, by Gary Soto. Copyright © 1985. This excerpt is used by permission of the author.

**23** "Mother," from THE SEVENTH CHILD, by Freddie Mae Baxter. Copyright © 1999 by Freddie Mae Baxter. Reprinted by permission of Alfred A. Knopf, a Division of Random House, Inc

**33** "The Great Whales," from WHALES, by Seymour Simon. Copyright © 1989 by Seymour Simon. Used by permission of HarperCollins Publishers.

**41** "Killer Whales," from KILLER WHALE, by Caroline Arnold. William Morrow & Company.

**51** "Joshua," from MY NAME IS AMERICA: THE JOURNAL OF JOSHUA LOPER, by Walter Dean Myers. Copyright © 1999 by Walter Dean Myers. Reprinted by permission of Scholastic Inc.

**59** "The Man," from SOMEWHERE IN THE DARKNESS, by Walter Dean Myers. Copyright © 1992 by Walter Dean Myers. Reprinted by permission of Scholastic Inc.

**69** "What Happened During the Ice Storm," by Jim Heynen.

**76** "Cheating," from FAMILY SECRETS, by Susan Shreve. Copyright © 1979 by Susan Shreve. Reprinted by permission of Alfred A. Knopf, a Division of Random House Inc.

**85** "Egyptian Mummies," from MUMMIES AND THEIR MYSTERIES, by Charlotte Wilcox. Copyright 1993 by Charlotte Wilcox. Published by Carolrhoda Books, Inc. Mpls., MN. Used by permission of the publisher. All rights reserved.

**93** "Mummies," from TALES MUMMIES TELL, by Patricia Lauber. HarperCollins.

**103, 112** "Summer Berries," from SWEETGRASS, by Jan Hudson. Copyright © 1989 by Jan Hudson. Used by permission of Philomel Books, a division of Penguin Putnam, Inc.

**123** "A Better Life," from SAMMY SOSA, A BIOGRAPHY, by Bill Gutman. Pocket/Simon & Schuster.

**132** "Jackie Robinson's First Game," from STEALING HOME: THE STORY OF JACKIE ROBINSON, by Barry Denenberg. Copyright © 1990 by Barry Denenberg. Reprinted by permission of Scholastic Inc.

**143** "The Strangers Arrive." Reprinted from THE LOST TEMPLE OF THE AZTECS by Shelly Tanaka. Text, design, and compilation © 1998 by The Madison Press Limited. Published by Hyperion Books for Children.

**153** "The Great Moctezuma," from THE AZTECS, by Donna Walsh Shepherd. Copyright © 1992 by Donna Walsh Shepherd.

**163** "I Am Miguel," from ...AND NOW MIGUEL, by Joseph Krumgold. Copyright © 1953 by Joseph Krumgold. Used by permission of HarperCollins Publishers.

**171** "Sangre de Cristo Mountains" from ...AND NOW MIGUEL, by Joseph Krumgold. Copyright © 1953 by Joseph Krumgold. Used by permission of HarperCollins Publishers.

**183** "Bradley Chalkers," from THERE'S A BOY IN THE GIRLS' BATHROOM, by Louis Sachar. Copyright © 1987 by Louis Sachar. Reprinted by permission of Alfred A. Knopf Children's Books, a division of Random House, Inc.

**191** "Sam Gribley," from ON THE FAR SIDE OF THE MOUNTAIN, by Jean Craighead George. Copyright © by Jean Craighead George. Used by permission of Dutton Children's Books, a division of Penguin Putnam Inc.

**203** "Buffalo Hunt." Reprinted from MY INDIAN BOYHOOD by Luther Standing Bear by permission of the University of Nebraska Press. Copyright 1931 by Luther Standing Bear. Copyright © renewed 1959 by May M. Jones.

**214** "The Sunflower Room," from REMEMBER MY NAME, by Sara H. Banks. Copyright © 1993 by Sara H. Banks. Reprinted by permission of The Court Wayne Press.

**225, 232** "Milo," from THE PHANTOM TOLLBOOTH, by Norton Juster, illustrated by Jules Feiffer. Copyright © 1961 by Norton Juster. Illustrations © 1961 by Jules Feiffer. Copyright renewed 1989 by Norton Juster. Illustrations copyright renewed 1989 by Jules Feiffer. Reprinted with permission of Random House Children's Books, a division of Random House, Inc.

**Photography:**

COVER: All photos © Eileen Ryan.

TABLE OF CONTENTS and INTRODUCTION: All photos © Eileen Ryan except where noted. Page 3: center—courtesy Library of Congress. Page 4: lower right—courtesy Library of Congress. Page 5: upper left, center left—courtesy Library of Congress.

CHAPTER 1: All photos © Eileen Ryan except where noted. Page 11: center—courtesy Library of Congress. Page 22: upper right—courtesy Library of Congress. Page 23: lower right—courtesy Library of Congress. Pages 24, 26: courtesy Library of Congress. Page 27: upper left—courtesy Library of Congress. Page 28: upper right—courtesy Library of Congress. Pages 29-30: courtesy Library of Congress.

CHAPTER 2: Page 31: top—© Eileen Ryan. Page 32: center— © Superstock. Page 38: top © Superstock. Page 44: © Superstock.

CHAPTER 3: All photos courtesy Library of Congress except where noted. Page 53: © Eileen Ryan. Page 58: background—© Eileen Ryan. Page 59: lower right—© Eileen Ryan. Page 60: © Eileen Ryan. Pages 62-65: backgrounds—© Eileen Ryan.

CHAPTER 4: All photos © Eileen Ryan except where noted. Page 67: bottom—courtesy Library of Congress. Pages 68-70, 72-74: courtesy Library of Congress.

CHAPTER 5: All photos courtesy Library of Congress except where noted. Page 84: upper right— © AP/Wideworld. Page 85: bottom—© AP/Wideworld. Page 86, 89: © Gianni Dagli Orti/Corbis. Page 93: © AP/Wideworld. Page 94: © George F. Mobley/National Geographic Society. Page 96: © Eileen Ryan. Page 98: bottom—© Eileen Ryan. Page 100: © AP/Wideworld.

## Acknowledgments continued

CHAPTER 6: All photos courtesy Library of Congress except where noted. Page 110: © Eileen Ryan.

CHAPTER 7: All photos courtesy Library of Congress except where noted. Page 121: lower right—© AP/Wideworld. Page 122: inset—© AP/Wideworld. Page 123: lower right—© Tom Bean/Corbis. Page 124: © Adam Woolfit/Corbis. Page 125: background—© Eileen Ryan, lower right—© Tom Bean/Corbis. Page 126: bottom—© Eileen Ryan. Page 127: background—© Adam Woolfit/Corbis, inset—© Eileen Ryan. Page 128: © Eileen Ryan. Page 129: inset—© AP/Wideworld. Page 135: inset—© Eileen Ryan. 138: background—© Eileen Ryan.

CHAPTER 8: All photos courtesy Library of Congress except where noted. Page 144: © Eileen Ryan. Pages 158, 160: © Eileen Ryan.

CHAPTER 9: All photos courtesy Library of Congress except where noted. Pages 164–165, 167–168: backgrounds—© Eileen Ryan.

CHAPTER 10: All photos © Eileen Ryan except where noted. Page 181: top—Ted Swen, courtesy U.S. Fish and Wildlife Service. Page 190: upper right—Craig Koppie, courtesy U.S. Fish and Wildlife Service. Page 193–194: Ted Swen, courtesy U.S. Fish and Wildlife Service. Page 195: Shawn Padgett, courtesy U.S. Fish and Wildlife Service. Page 196: Ron Singer, courtesy U.S. Fish and Wildlife Service. Page 197: courtesy U.S. Fish and Wildlife Service. Page 198: Ted Swen, courtesy U.S. Fish and Wildlife Service. Page 200: Ted Swen and Shawn Padgett, courtesy U.S. Fish and Wildlife Service.

CHAPTER 11: All photos courtesy Library of Congress except where noted. Page 204: inset—© Eileen Ryan.

CHAPTER 12: All photos © Eileen Ryan.

**Cover and Book Design:** Christine Ronan and Sean O'Neill, Ronan Design

**Permissions:**
Feldman and Associates
**Developed by Nieman Inc.**

*The editors have made every effort to trace the ownership of all copyrighted selections found in this book and to make full acknowledgment for their use. Omissions brought to our attention will be corrected in a subsequent edition.*

## Author/Title Index